COSMOPOLITAN LOVE

COSMOPOLITAN LOVE

Utopian Vision in D. H. Lawrence and Eileen Chang

Sijia Yao

UNIVERSITY OF MICHIGAN PRESS

Ann Arbor

For questions or permissions, please contact um.press.perms@umich.edu

Published in the United States of America by the
University of Michigan Press
Printed and bound by CPI Group (UK) Ltd, Croydon, CR0 4YY

First published November 2023

A CIP catalog record for this book is available from the British Library.

Library of Congress Cataloging-in-Publication Data

Names: Sijia, Yao, author.
Title: Cosmopolitan love : utopian vision in D.H. Lawrence and Eileen Chang / Yao Sijia.
Other titles: Utopian vision in D.H. Lawrence and Eileen Chang
Description: Ann Arbor [Michigan] : University of Michigan Press, 2023. | Includes
    bibliographical references (pages 143–151) and index. | English text with some passages
    in Chinese with English translation.
Identifiers: LCCN 2023023174 (print) | LCCN 2023023175 (ebook) | ISBN 9780472076536
    (hardcover) | ISBN 9780472056538 (paperback) | ISBN 9780472903931 (ebook other)
Subjects: LCSH: Lawrence, D. H. (David Herbert), 1885–1930—Criticism and
    interpretation. | Zhang, Ailing—Criticism and interpretation. | Cosmopolitanism in
    literature. | Transnationalism in literature. | Love in literature. | Sex in literature.
Classification: LCC PN56.C683 S55 2023 (print) | LCC PN56.C683 (ebook) |
    DDC 823/.912—dc23/eng/20230725
LC record available at https://lccn.loc.gov/2023023174
LC ebook record available at https://lccn.loc.gov/2023023175

DOI: https://doi.org/10.3998/mpub.12392047

The University of Michigan Press's open access publishing program is made possible
thanks to additional funding from the University of Michigan Office of the Provost and the
generous support of contributing libraries

Cover illustration: *Resonant Tone to the Mountain and up to the Moon* (*Liaoliang yisheng
shanyue gao* 嘹亮一声山月高), by Zikai Feng (丰子恺 1898–1975). Courtesy of China
International Auction Co., Ltd.

For my parents

Acknowledgments

If a book has its own life, writing is creating a new life. I would like to thank the Lynn Research Fellowship, the Purdue Research Foundation, the Purdue Promise Award, the Research Impact and Engagement Grant at the University of Nebraska–Lincoln, and Soka University of America for their funding and support during the development of this project. The introduction includes material that previously appeared as "Third Term Comparison" in *Telos* 199 (Summer 2022). I am grateful to Telos Press Publishing for permission to reproduce it here. In addition, chapter 2 includes material from my essay "Female Desire: Defiant Text and Intercultural Context in Works by D. H. Lawrence and Eileen Chang" in *Rocky Mountain Review of Language and Literature* 71, no. 2 (2017), and I thank the Rocky Mountain Modern Language Association for permission to draw on my essay for this book.

I want to extend my sincere gratitude to my mentors, colleagues, and friends who read, listened to, and commented on my project: my adviser, Charles Ross; my dissertation committee members, Daniel Hsieh, Jennifer Freeman Marshall, and Hongjian Wang; my mentors and friends at the University of Nebraska–Lincoln, Parks Coble, Patty Simpson, and Ikuho Amano, and a number of scholars in the field who showed their persistent support and friendship, Thomas O. Beebee, Rey Chow, Keith Cushman, Wei Hong, Ying Hu, Xinmin Liu, Christopher Lupke, Paul Manfredi, David Pan, and Jiwei Xiao. I am deeply grateful to Christopher Dreyer, acquisitions editor at the University of Michigan Press, for working closely with me on publishing my manuscript and obtaining the funding for open access to the book. I would also like to thank the wonderful staff at the Press including Kevin Rennells, Anne Taylor, and Devon Thomas. This book is my tribute to my parents and family, whom I love deeply and cherish dearly. I am so grateful for the love and understanding they have unconditionally provided for my growth as a daughter, a scholar, and an individual with the courage and freedom to choose a life of my own.

Contents

Introduction

I can only write what I feel pretty strongly about: and that, at present, is the relations between men and women. After all, it is *the* problem of today, the establishment of a new relation, or the readjustment of the old one, between men and women.
    —D. H. Lawrence, Letter to Garnett, May 1913[1]

And, in fact, all I really write about are some of the trivial things that happen between men and women. There is no war and no revolution in my works. I think that people are more straightforward and unguarded in love than they are in war or revolution.
    —Eileen Chang, "Writing of One's Own," 1944[2]

我甚至只是寫些男女間的小事情，我的作品裏沒有戰爭，也沒有革命。我以為人在戀愛的時候，是比在戰爭或革命的時候更素樸，也更放恣的。
    —張愛玲，《自己的文章》1944年

Love as a feeling is universal. Since we all have a sense for what it means, this default understanding of love is as deeply rooted and unconsciously ingrained in us as our relationship to our own family. Consequently, we are too familiar with it to be able to step back and really observe its form and significance. To really see what love is would require us to step outside of ourselves, as if we had been born in a different time and place. It is only through approaching love in a drastically different cultural system that we are able to truly see the real picture of love in our own mind as well as in the minds of others. To understand love requires a comparison, and to understand the ideas of Chinese love and Western love we need to step out of the confines of each tradition to compare how the concept of love emerged and developed in distinct ways in each context.

In the Western tradition, Plato defines love (*éros*) as the "desire for the perpetual possession of the good" in *The Symposium*, and Aristotle discusses friendship (*philía*) in his *Nicomachean Ethics*.[3] They thereby establish an important place for love within an overall metaphysical and political framework. As C. S. Lewis notes, Plato's *éros*, philosophical and transcendental, mounts the ladder ascending to the divine, and he idealizes love as "goodness" and "absolute beauty." One reaches the higher rungs by leaving the lower ones behind: "We find the conception of a ladder whereby the soul may ascend from human love to divine. . . . The original object of human love has simply fallen out of sight before the soul arrives at the spiritual object."[4] Drawing on the Greek tradition, Christianity placed love at the center of its metaphysical framework by establishing love as the key characteristic of the divine. Since God is love in this conception, Christian love, divine and metaphysical, eradicates carnal desire and primitive thoughts.

In the later tradition of medieval courtly love beginning in the twelfth century and romantic love starting in the seventeenth century, love becomes increasingly detached from the metaphysical context, even though courtly and romantic love depend upon Christian tropes to maintain an intensity of the love relationship. The development of romantic love out of a Christian conception of sacrifice maintains the centrality of love for emotional life, transferring transcendence into the experience of a romantic couple. Denis de Rougemont traces the evolution of romantic love, arguing that passionate love afflicts, and simultaneously elevates, human beings. By examining famous literary texts in the West starting from the legend of Tristan and Isolde, he posits that suffering, obstruction, and death thwart passion but, at the same time, foster and ennoble romantic love. De Rougement points out that romance is the parting of the lovers. What the lovers "need is not one another's presence, but one another's absence. Thus, the partings of the lovers are dictated by their passion itself, and by the love they bestow on their passion rather than on its satisfaction or on its living object. That is why the Romance abounds in obstructions."[5] In the end, romance requires death for its perfect triumph, climax, and fulfillment. The absence of the lover stirs, fosters, and glorifies the feeling of love by linking it to sacrifice and renunciation.

As Niklas Luhmann describes, by the nineteenth and early twentieth centuries, love as passion within the pair-bond comes to dominate Western emotional life and its reconstruction of society based on these individual relationships.[6] If romantic love ennobles such relationships, bridging the gap between sex and love,[7] the detachment of love from Christianity's metaphysical framework also led later to a focus on individual desire rather than the sacrificial ideals of Christianity, leading to Sigmund Freud's derivation of love from sexual desire. Freud argues that love is sublimated as "overvaluation" when sex is inhibited,[8] asserting thereby, like prior philosophers such as Schopenhauer, the determining role of sex.

The general development up until the early twentieth century is thus one in which a philosophical focus on the link between love and a metaphysical conception of the good develops out of the Greek tradition, leading in Christianity to a focus on love as the key form of both human and divine relationship. Coming out of the Middle Ages, the idea of romantic love gained intensity through its borrowing from religious tropes while eventually casting off the metaphysical framework in order to focus on individual desires and aspirations within a romantic couple. By the early twentieth century, love had maintained its centrality for social life while losing its metaphysical significance.

In China, in contrast to Western thinking, the subject of love has been mostly overlooked and dismissed as a feminine, trivial topic barely worthy of study compared to such masculine discourses as history, politics, nationalism, and morality. Love, called *qing* 情 (sentiment, emotion), broadly refers to any deep and genuine emotions. Like that of Western love, the definition of *qing* has varied over time in Chinese history. The cult of *qing* started the major revolution of the heart in Chinese literature, which can be traced back to the late Ming dynasty.[9] Since that time, *qing* has gained increasing attention from Chinese literati and attracted the spotlight in such popular literary genres as the play and the novel. Tang Xianzu 湯顯祖 (1550–1616), a playwright writing at the same time as Shakespeare, mystified *qing* as a primitive but simultaneously transcendental force in his death-love play *Mudan ting* 牡丹亭 (*The Peony Pavilion*). Feng Menglong 馮夢龍 (1574–1646), a Chinese literary scholar, categorized his 850 collected Chinese love tales into twenty-four types and eventually compiled them into an anthology: *Qing shi lei lue* 情史類略 (*Qing Categorized Records*). Cao Xueqin's 曹雪芹 (ca. 1715–ca. 1763) *Honglou meng* 紅樓夢 (*The Dream of the Red Mansion* or *The Story of the Stone*) in the Qing dynasty further explored human emotions that could be elevated over politics, orthodoxy, or morality. As these examples illustrate, the idea of the cult of *qing* approximates what is referred to as "love" in the West.[10]

However, in general, Chinese orthodox intellectuals considered love as an inappropriate subject in literature and society. In China, *wen* 文 (literature) has always played a defining role in politics and social order. Literati in traditional China had been the backbone of the central and local governments that bolstered the absolute power of imperial rulers dynasty after dynasty. Therefore, literature had been highly politicized and utilized to serve the state, creating a culture that devalued the private. The feeling of *qing* was strictly limited within the inferior literary genres, such as *ci* poetry, folk stories, drama, and novels. Thus, they failed to carry as much weight as in the central elite forms of parallel prose and essays. Even if love appears in the orthodox classics, it was either ignored or interpreted away. For instance, a number of love poems in *Shijing* 詩經 (*Book of Poetry*, the oldest collection of Chinese poems, composed from the eleventh to seventh centuries BC) were reinterpreted as moral and political texts by Confucians, reducing it to an orthodox Chinese classic that only served the state and the political order. Love poems composed in later dynasties were similarly subjected to social and political causes. Commentators held that the idea of love merely expressed the poets' loyalty for the emperor or patriotism to the country. According to this view, poets may have disguised themselves as a lonely or abandoned lady in the poem, but in fact they were lamenting their destiny or expressing their passion for politics. The classical Chinese literary interpretation of the canon had marginalized and barred love and sexuality for thousands of years.

As a consequence, Denis de Rougemont and Irving Singer contend that romantic love is absent in China.[11] Indeed, unlike Western writers, such as Plato, Sappho, Ovid, Dante, Spenser, Shelly, and Shakespeare, most Chinese intellectuals either subconsciously overlooked or intentionally evaded the topic of love in their literary canon. In the twelfth century, China had no literary equivalents to *Tristan and Isolde*. There were also barely any Chinese writers claiming the sublimity of love, such as when Emily Dickinson focuses so intently on love and death in the nineteenth century. Nevertheless, the assertion that love only exists in the West is certainly a distortion.

In China, love undoubtedly exists but has not played an important role in religious or political thought in the same way as love in the West established through Christianity, the foundation for both divine and human relationships. The difference can be summed up in the way in which political and metaphysical concerns were managed in the European Middle Ages through the relationship between the Holy Roman emperor and the Christian pope, while in China the emperor combined the political and metaphysical aspects in one figure referred to as the Son of Heaven.

Nevertheless, by the beginning of the twentieth century, there was a convergence in the two very separate traditions to the extent that love in the West had become decoupled from religion and reduced to a private affair while love in China was still sidelined within the bounds of the private sphere. In this modern context, the key innovation consisted of exploring the link between love and a public sphere of both political and metaphysical matters. It was at this point that a writer from England and a writer from China could be pursuing the common project of focusing on love as the foundation for the transformation of social life and a renewed metaphysical perspective on the world. This project links the works of D. H. (David Herbert) Lawrence (1885–1930) and Eileen Chang (Ailing Zhang 張愛玲, 1920–95). Both engaged in an intense exploration of love in a way that sought to reveal its significance as a basis for change, leading to a cosmopolitan attitude.

Lawrence, the son of a working-class English miner, ascended to intellectual circles through education and persistent literary pursuit in the first decades of the twentieth century. In his work, he challenged the rigid social order in England and attempted to destabilize the wave of capitalist modernization. Dissatisfied with a limited national vision, Lawrence was always on the move from England, Germany, Italy, and Switzerland to Australia, the United States, and France. His love stories, *Sons and Lovers*, *Women in Love*, and *Lady Chatterley's Lover*, to name a few, also extended a social critique of England from the private to the public with a cosmopolitan vision.

Eileen Chang, an aristocratic Chinese woman, presented Chinese heterosexual love roughly forty years later, when she witnessed the old world rotting and dying and simultaneously the new world desperately crawling toward enlightened, modern China from political chaos and the Sino-Japanese War. Born to a distinguished aristocratic family in 1920s China, Chang was caught between two worlds: the traditional Chinese and the modern Western.[12] Her father educated her in the culture of classical Chinese poetry and novels, while her mother, who chose to further her study overseas and finally divorced Chang's father, influenced Chang with progressive Western thoughts and beliefs. In the 1940s, Chang won millions of readers in Shanghai. Nevertheless, she was never considered as a serious writer because her works dealt with women and love, topics that Chinese critics considered decadent and trivial. Chang shared the same experience with women writers ranging from Charlotte Brontë to Toni Morrison with regard to public reception. Pursuing a literary autonomy, she left Shanghai for Hong Kong in 1952 and migrated to the United States in 1955, hoping to become a successful world-class writer. She had been a migrant writer but then descended into gray oblivion in America.

Although there is a temporal discrepancy of several decades between the two authors, they both address similar historical contexts of modernization in a time of growing connections between the East and the West in the twentieth century. Other scholars have for the most part compared Eileen Chang to her female European counterparts, such as Katherine Mansfield, Virginia Woolf, and George Eliot, without inquiring into the details of Chang's conception of love. Discussions of Lawrence have not compared his work with that of Chang. Yet, a common purpose drives Lawrence and Chang to create a notion of love that directly critiques historical limitations without offering a crystalized solution. Both writers intend to cross their national boundaries to embrace a cosmopolitan identity by departing from their home cultures, physically and mentally. The comparison between these two writers opens onto an alternative version of cosmopolitanism, a cosmopolitan sensibility, that can be practiced by individuals, rather than state administrations or communal traditions, in both the East and the West. This study closely examines and compares the social and political consequences of their ideas of love by linking their conceptions of love to questions of modernization and cosmopolitanism in order to understand how Lawrence and Chang independently developed a similar modern conception of love that establishes a basis for new kinds of social relationships.

Reception of Lawrence and Chang

The social aspect of Lawrence's and Chang's works generally has not been appreciated in the reception of their work. Having declined in prominence, Lawrence and Chang were both recovered by renowned scholars in the 1960s. However, the idea of love in both writers has been surprisingly neglected and understudied despite the fact that Lawrence regarded himself as the "priest of love"[13] and Chang publicly declared her primary literary interest to be "the trivial things that happen between men and women."[14] In the twenty-first century, Lawrence's literary reputation is actually less secure than that of Chang. Unlike Chang, Lawrence, now considered obsolete, is known as a contributor to sexual liberation and the man who worships the phallus. Chang's pithy, elegant, and subtle statements are very different from Lawrence's mocking fury. Nevertheless, both authors write exclusively on relations between men and women, which have been easily belittled and overlooked in readings.

Lawrence's ideas of sexuality and heterosexual relations aroused controversies among moralists and radical feminists over the course of the twentieth century, thereby overshadowing a possible reading of love. The banning of *The Rainbow* and the trial concerning *Lady Chatterley's Lover* aroused political debates about censorship and the legitimacy of explicit sexuality. He is either condemned as a pornographer or as a defender of patriarchy or elevated as the "exciting prophet of the sexual revolution" and "the apostle of traditional humanism."[15] Either way, Lawrence's central heresy is primarily about sex. As Frank Kermode suggests in *Lawrence*, "Sexual reform is the key to cultural and economic reform," and it is Lawrence who prefigured the sexual liberation in the 1960s.[16]

Lawrence was harshly attacked by feminists such as Kate Millett and Simone de Beauvoir. The former reviled Lawrence as a misogynistic sexual politician,[17] while the latter repudiated Lawrence's notions as a form of "phallic" superiority that perpetuates a stereotypical representation of women.[18] Hilary Simpson believed that Lawrence insists on male supremacy and feminine submission.[19] Feminism in the 1970s and 1980s further attacked Lawrence as a monolithic masculine monster. Lerner observes, "A good deal has conspired to undermine Lawrence's reputation [. . .] and nothing more than the rise of feminist criticism."[20] By contrast, F. R. Leavis devoted tremendous critical efforts to "win clear recognition for the nature of Lawrence's greatness."[21] He highly praised Lawrence's love stories, such as *Rainbow* and *Women in Love*, as the greatest art. Michael Black, Leavis's follower, published four excellent books on Lawrence.[22] Kingsley Widmer justifies Lawrence's sexual desire as a defiant, radical challenge to society, proposing that Lawrence uses desire to affirm rather than negate life. Mark Spilka argues that "Lawrence was a religious artist, and that all his work was governed by religious ends."[23] Linda Ruth Williams combines these arguments and claims that Lawrence is "both sexual liberator *and* high puritan."[24] The divided literary reception of Lawrence constantly feeds Lawrence studies and maintains his canonical position in the long run.[25] Even though these scholars focus on the themes of sexuality, feminism, and aesthetics, they in fact do not devote attention to the theme of love, which is Lawrence's primary interest.

There is also a split in the established critical understanding about Chang. She has been derided as a popular romance writer, and at times her focus on love therefore barely attracted any attention. By contrast, literary elites in recent decades starting with C. T. Hsia have placed her in literary studies rather than within a larger sociopolitical dimension. She was undervalued as merely "a banal boudoir realist" in China due to her use of domestic settings and focus on female subjectivity.[26] In the 1940s, China was undergoing Japanese invasion (1937–45) and an endless civil war. Chang gained her popularity by writing about middle-class domestic life and love affairs in Japanese-occupied Shanghai. However, most of the Chinese writers in China during that special political time advocated the May Fourth ideology, embracing science and democracy. Leftist writers promoted revolutionary literature to gain their nation's freedom and independence, and their ethos was that everything, including private life, should be subordinated to the national cause. Nationalists, and later communists, excluded her from the literary canon, which considered literature to be subordinate to the state.[27]

Despite this disapproval, Chang occupies an important place in modern Chinese literary history nowadays. The restoration of her literary fame owes debts to critics such as C. T. Hsia, David Der-wei Wang,[28] Leo Ou-fan Lee, Nicole Huang, Ling Ke,[29] Wenbiao Tang,[30] and Zishan Chen[31] as well as numerous scholars from Taiwan, Hong Kong, and mainland China.[32] In 1961, Hsia anthologized Chang in his groundbreaking book, *A History of Modern Chinese Fiction*. Closely examining Chang's major literary works, "The Golden Cangue," "Jasmine Tea," "Blockade," and *The Rice Sprout Song*, Hsia praises Chang's contribution to modern Chinese literature: "Eileen Chang is not only the best and most important writer in Chinese today; her short stories alone invite valid comparisons with, and in some respects claim superiority over, the work of serious modern women writers in English: Katherine Mansfield, Katherine Anne Porter, Eudora Welty, and Carson McCullers."[33] Chang became a canonical heroine through the work of Hsia. The Chang fever in Taiwan, Hong Kong, and mainland China in the 1990s marked the beginning of the rise of her fame.[34] The excellence of Chang's literature was sanctified by the author's death, and her works recently have been anthologized by the two authoritative publications *The Norton Anthology of World Literature*[35] and *The Longman Anthology: World Literature*.[36] Her story "Lust, Caution" inspired a Hollywood film in 2007, directed by the Oscar-winning director Ang Lee and drawing public attention to Chang all over the world.

The reception history of Chang's literary reputation, as in Lawrence's case, encapsulates the historical stages of her local condition.[37] China underwent a dramatic transition from Confucian feudal society to the semicolonized modern world, from suppression of humanity to the revolution of the heart, with love demonstrating the most intensive states of human existence. As Haiyan Lee insists, "Discourses of sentiment are not merely representations or expressions of inner emotions, but articulatory practices that participate in (re)defining the social order and (re) producing forms of self and sociality. Emotion talk is never about emotion pure and simple, but is always also about something else, namely, identity, morality, gender, author, power and community."[38] And yet, Chang was either trivialized for her narrow interest in love, marriage, and domestic space or elevated for her sophisticated, inventive aesthetics and feminist, modernist perspective.

The approaches to Lawrence and Chang reflect the specific historical backdrops in their respective cultures, which explains the prevalent Western misreading of Lawrence's love and the Chinese demeaning of Chang's love. In analogous ways, both writers have been either criticized for their inability to properly address social and political issues or praised for their exclusive focus on personal relationships. Interpretations of Lawrence and Chang consequently have not been able to come to terms with the social significance of their works, and the shared idea of love has often been downplayed, understudied, and imprisoned in its private attic.

Yet, the sexual love in Lawrence is framed as a rebellion against Victorian orthodoxy and traditions that define Englishness and national identity. Likewise, Eileen Chang's sexual love, though not so victorious and affirmative as Lawrence's, also challenges the dominant discourses on national belonging, be it Confucian traditions that advocate hierarchical stability or nationalistic slogans that use free love to start the revolution. Their conceptions of love address not simply personal issues but also social relationships in local and nation-state contexts, as well as global and cosmic ones, through subversion, defiance, and detachment.

Utopia in China and the West

To emancipate the power of love from the private into the public, the two writers adopted love as the form of their engagement in an alternative utopian freedom that transgresses and transcends local, national, global, and even cosmic boundaries. In a letter to his friend, Lawrence explicitly addresses his strong interest in the love relations between men and women: "I can only write what I feel pretty strongly about: and that, at present, is the relations between men and women. After all, it is *the* problem of today, the establishment of a new relation, or the re-adjustment of the old one, between men and women."[39] For Lawrence, "the relations between men and women" was "the problem" of his time, when dramatic changes happened in the form of problematic local culture, war, industrialization, or the death of God. The love relation as the basic unit of social relation in private becomes a crucial source from which all the bigger issues in public originate. Lawrence's approach to love in the beginning carries a strong sense of sociopolitical engagement.

His voice, as Keith Cushman and Dennis Jackson put it, is "one of the strongest" in twentieth-century literature, and they refer to Lawrence as the "great enemy of complacency, spurring us to ask difficult questions about love and power, about the society we have constructed, about the mysterious universe we inhabit, above all about ourselves."[40] Indeed, Lawrence engages in the sociopolitical discussions and philosophical pursuits in his lifetime by devoting his fiction writing to interpersonal relations in domestic settings. His defiance, or insolence in many people's eyes, is connected with metaphysical reinvention as well as skepticism against dominant cultural conceptions in the early twentieth century.

Over three decades later, Eileen Chang wrote in one of her prose pieces: "And, in fact, all I really write about are some of the trivial things that happen between men and women. There is no war and no revolution in my works. I think that people are more straightforward and unguarded in love than they are in war or revolution."[41] As opposed to Lawrence's self-conscious use of love to revolutionize society, Chang explicitly expresses her indifference to social engagement and maintains an apolitical stance. Her absolute indulgence in "trivial" relationships can easily lead those nationalists and reformists to categorize her as a middle-brow popular writer. However, this pure denouncement of politics and sheer distance from social engagement paradoxically highlight the very fact that her writings radically transform readers' understandings of Chinese tradition, nationalism, modernity, and faith in this period when China quickly underwent the process of modernization and Westernization. This negation of sociopolitical engagement actually strikes the very basic note of her lifelong literary production: negative utopia. Chang's depiction of the bleak realities of a modern existence can be contrasted with a frustrated, decadent, but defiant love.[42] Contrary to Chang's negative utopia, Lawrence envisions an alternative sociopolitical utopia affirmatively and optimistically. Yet, regardless of their distinctive proposed utopian existences, both Lawrence and Chang attempt to seek an alternative utopia to orient their engagement with local culture, globalized modernization, and eventually cosmic enlightenment. Highly aware of an apocalyptic future, both writers are driven by a desire to discover an alternative utopia.

Harold Bloom has praised Lawrence by citing a "celebratory passage [that] moves rapidly into an ecstasy of heroic vitalism, transcending the Zarathustra of Nietzsche and the related reveries of Pater in the 'Conclusion' to *The Renaissance*."[43] The voluptuous passage Bloom has in mind is worth citing in its entirety, because it stirs one's spiritual being as much as the most passionate sermon does. In it, Lawrence says that the new faith he worships is "to be alive." And the sign of life for Lawrence is "passionate love." Any of Lawrence's contradictory ideas or offensive statements could be pardoned, given the omniscient and omnipotent god–like power incarnated in this paragraph, which touches the very depth of our hearts and inspires us to persistently pursue the true meaning of a modern existence as a utopian vision:

> But the Apocalypse shows, by its very resistance, the things that the human heart secretly yearns after. By the very frenzy with which the Apocalypse destroys the sun and the stars, the world, and all kings and all rulers, all scarlet and purple and cinnamon, all harlots, finally all men altogether who are not "sealed," we can see how deeply the apocalyptists are yearning for the sun and the stars and the earth and the waters of the earth, for nobility and lordship and might, and scarlet and gold splendour, for passionate love, and a proper unison with men, apart from this sealing business. What man most passionately wants is his living wholeness and his living unison, not his own isolate salvation of his "soul." Man wants his physical fulfilment first and foremost, since now, once and once only, he is in the flesh and potent. For man, the vast marvel is to be alive. For man, as for flower and beast and bird, the supreme triumph is to be most vividly, most perfectly alive. Whatever the unborn and the dead may know, they cannot know the beauty, the marvel of being alive in the flesh. The dead may look after the afterwards. But the magnificent here and now of life in the flesh is ours, and ours alone, and ours only for a time. We ought to dance with rapture that we should be alive and in the flesh, and part of the living, incarnate cosmos. I am part of the sun as my eye is part of me. That I am part of the earth my feet know perfectly, and my blood is

part of the sea. My soul knows that I am part of the human race, my soul is an organic part of the great human soul, as my spirit is part of my nation. In my own very self, I am part of my family. There is nothing of me that is alone and absolute except my mind, and we shall find that the mind has no existence by itself, it is only the glitter of the sun on the surface of the waters.

So that my individualism is really an illusion. I am a part of the great whole, and I can never escape. But I *can* deny my connections, break them, and become a fragment. Then I am wretched.

What we want is to destroy our false, inorganic connections, especially those related to money, and re-establish the living organic connections, with the cosmos, the sun and earth, with mankind and nation and family. Start with the sun, and the rest will slowly, slowly happen.[44]

When we envision the modern future in the apocalypse, we foresee the desolation and death ahead of us. The apocalyptic violence and negation of life drive our "yearning for the sun and the stars and the earth and the waters of the earth, for nobility and lordship and might, and scarlet and gold splendour, for passionate love, and a proper unison with men, apart from this sealing business." His response to the apocalypse is "to be alive." He considers the aliveness "in the flesh" as a "vast marvel." Life becomes miraculous when the human recognizes the cosmos in the body. "I am part of the sun as my eye is part of me." The body as "part of the living" incarnates cosmos, thereby organically integrating our limited human existence into the vast and permanent universe. He defamiliarizes and deifies a secular existence by elevating it to the marvel and taking down the cosmos to embody it in the flesh. This redemption to claim a primal existence reformulates a new connection between the earth and the ultimate, thereby releasing a primitive power that can counter the dominant falsehood. Lawrence attempts to "destroy our false, inorganic connections" through love and "re-establish the living organic connections" with "family," "nation," and "the cosmos." Lawrence's assertion of aliveness and organic connection vigorously resists the apocalyptic wasteland of fragmented modernization.

If Lawrence embraces his utopia affirmatively and heroically, Chang pursues her utopia by negating it and primarily dwelling on the suffocating, deathly modern realities. Chang was also exposed to devastating realities in a society imbued with chaos and wars. She shared a similar apocalyptic view about life and universe but did so in a more pessimistic lamentation in comparison to Lawrence's extraordinary heroic vitalism:

> Even if I were able to wait, the times rush impatiently forward—already in the midst of destruction, with a still-greater destruction yet to come. There will come a day when our civilization, whether sublime or frivolous, will be a thing of the past. If the word I use the most in my writing is "desolation," that is because this troubling premonition underlies all my thinking.[45]

> 個人即使等得及，時代是倉卒的，已經在破壞中，還有更大的破壞要來。有一天我們的文明，不論是昇華還是浮華，都要成為過去。如果我最常用的字是「荒涼」，那是因為思想背景裏有這惘惘的威脅。[46]

Chang was expecting catastrophe when China was rolling extremely quickly into modernity. Chang, different from Lawrence's aggressive initiation of a new world order, pessimistically waited for the destruction and vicariously transformed this anxiety into her art. Her apocalyptic voice, the voice of desolation, penetrates every page of her love stories. Her pessimism is as strong a critique of the external world as Lawrence's heroic triumph.

Both Lawrence and Chang, therefore, tap the potentiality of love that could offer alternative understandings of their own societies under the conditions of modernism and cultural globalization. This extraordinary resemblance might derive from Chang's individualism, a mark of Western modernism, as well as from Lawrence's distance from Western orthodoxy. In his later career, Lawrence resorted to Eastern philosophy and pre-Christian existence. They also presented utterly different pictures of modernism from their contemporary modern peers. Lawrence never fit into the dominant trend of modernism endorsed by such authoritative figures as T. S. Eliot, Virginia Woolf, and James Joyce. Likewise, Chang also never went along with the prevalent modern ideas, strongly related to nationalism and revolution in the first half of twentieth-century China.

The difference between Lawrence's positive vision of utopia and Chang's negative one lies in the cultural contexts from which they begin. Lawrence could take advantage of the long tradition of meditation and writing about the concept of love as a metaphysical relationship, and his description of apocalypse and utopia brings earthly existence back into the realm of transcendence, based on a Christian trope of redemption. Chang, by contrast, working within a Chinese tradition that suppresses and marginalizes love, could not rely on a similar elevation of love, and her yearning for utopia is expressed negatively, as a momentary projection from out of the desolation that she confines herself to describing.

In response to the transition of their times, both writers offered an alternative mode of modernism in which to seek a realm of cosmopolitan freedom. Lawrence was living in the collapse of the Victorian era and at the beginning of the Modernist one, while Chang was torn between Confucianism, patriotic nationalism, and Western ideologies of modernism. China took a great jump from a feudal empire to an industrial society in the early twentieth century. Thus, Chang's and Lawrence's stories, as cultural products, reflect similar individualist reactions to dramatic social changes in differing cultural contexts. Despite a time interval between the two authors, they share the same pattern of a cosmopolitan love to engage with the world. Confronted with the modern revolutions in the areas of heart, politics, modernization, and religion, both Lawrence and Chang adopted love as a countercultural force to resist and critique local and global hegemonic discourses in order to predict a catastrophic future but simultaneously to propose an alternative approach to utopia. They both interpreted love as "powerful ideology," in the sociologist Mike Featherstone's term, to seek the truth about humanity, society, history, and culture.[47] They produced love stories in a revolutionary time of local transformation and global modernism, when texts and authors were on the move, to closely connect the individual with a realm of freedom, be it a cosmopolitan ideal or an ultimately cosmic transcendence.

The Idea of Cosmopolitan Love

The comparison of Lawrence and Chang aims not just to reread Lawrence and restore his literary glory by establishing his connections to the world of Chang but to rediscover the overlooked but commonly shared love in their literatures in order to address the lasting problems of today: cosmopolitanism that is defined by its opposite, that is, traditions, nationalism, mechanical teleological progress, and post-religion's faithlessness. Their works offer a perspective on the kind of political cosmopolitanism that Immanuel Kant suggested as a model for global peace and freedom based on rational political structures.[48] The focus of Kant's form of cosmopolitanism, put forward in one version by David Held,[49] is the establishment of a global form of justice that sets itself against both local attachments and local bonds. This approach treats love as something that must be suppressed to make way for a universal morality that does not establish preferences for one set of people over another. For Held, the goal is to establish global institutions such as international courts that would subordinate bonds of loyalty to a justice system that treats all of humanity equally. Similarly, Ulrich Beck describes a "cosmopolitan vision" in which transnational movements and relationships create a new type of economic and political structure for global order that transcends ethnic differences.[50] This movement from ethnic conflict to a serene vision attempts to suppress love, as expressed in the form of local bonds and nationalist fervor, in order to establish a cosmopolitan order.

As Martha Nussbaum argues, however, Kant's general attitude toward the passions prevents him from developing concrete proposals for moving toward a cosmopolitanism that addresses passions such as hate and anger: "Kant appears throughout his career to conceive of the passions including aggression, as natural, precultural, and not removable from human nature."[51] Because Kant sees passions as innate, his cosmopolitan project requires the suppression of passions and inclinations. Nussbaum revises this approach by describing a Stoic form of cosmopolitanism that derives from Cicero, Seneca, and Marcus Aurelius, in which the goal is not to suppress passions but to enlighten them through a training process: "Because these passions are not a part of the soul apart from thought but rather a certain sort of (misguided) thought, they can themselves be enlightened."[52] The Stoics propose that we make our passions fit with cosmopolitanism by reflecting upon our emotional responses in order to determine whether they are rational and then training ourselves to let go of anger, for instance. If the Stoics seek a training that removes certain passions such as anger, Nussbaum leans toward Aristotle's view that anger need not be eliminated. The passions can be altered so that they select the right objects. We can accordingly establish a cosmopolitan ethic in practice by educating our children so that they experience anger at cases of injustice, thereby enlightening the passions. Nussbaum thus reconciles passion with cosmopolitanism by seeing passion as the result of a thought process and thus subject to education and enlightenment.

Nevertheless, Nussbaum has a second alternative approach to cosmopolitanism when she considers love. For her, love is different from thought, almost the opposite, and consequently not open to influence through an education process. In describing the way in which cosmopolitanism and love are related, she does not present the idea that love, like hate and anger, could be channeled into directions that promote universal justice. Instead, there seems to be an opposition: "If one begins life as a child who loves and trusts his or her parents, it is tempting to want to reconstruct citizenship along the same lines, finding in an idealized image of a nation a surrogate parent who will do one's thinking for one. Cosmopolitanism offers no such refuge; it offers only reason and the love of humanity, which may seem at times less colorful than other sources of belonging."[53] Nationalism becomes an unthinking loyalty to the familiar.[54] By setting love for one's parents in opposition to both reason and love for humanity, Nussbaum indicates that cosmopolitanism must deny particular loves in order to move toward an ideal of justice that condemns favoritism.

However, love is essentially grounded in a willfulness that is opposed to the universal. It is this voluntary and exceptional aspect that renders love meaningful and valuable. Consequently, since the idea of love for humanity removes this favoritism, it undermines the willful aspect of love. Love is important precisely because it is not mandated, and a notion of cosmopolitan love must distinguish itself from a generalized love for humanity in order to retain the value of love as a voluntary rather than a dutiful act. Such an approach emancipates love from the parent-child relationship. Family love is not limited to the parent-child relationship but in fact will always involve a shift in the child's focus on the parent to the focus on a romance that brings the child outside the family (see chap. 1). This dynamic aspect in both love and the family links them to cosmopolitanism. Nussbaum overlooks the dynamics of love by limiting her conception of love to the love of a child for the parents and then treating the nation as "a surrogate parent who will do one's thinking for one." For Nussbaum, love has no independent standing as a value, lacking voluntary will and transformative power.[55]

Rather than setting justice against love and the cosmopolitan against the local, the idea of a cosmopolitan love would recognize the significance of love's willful logic as its way of lending particular significance to relationships. Such an approach allows us to examine the possibility of a cosmopolitanism that would require not a subordination of love but its assertive extension as a means of transforming relationships. One way to reconcile such love relationships with cosmopolitanism would be to reject Held's form of a political cosmopolitanism that establishes global institutions in order to pursue what David Miller has described as a moral cosmopolitanism, which demonstrates an equal moral concern for all humans without requiring an equal treatment.[56] This moral cosmopolitanism maintains a general attitude of concern for all of humanity while recognizing the intrinsic value of family and national bonds that justifies and requires special treatment between family members and members of a nation.

Kwame Anthony Appiah develops this idea of moral cosmopolitanism by being less ambitious and practically choosing to affect personal attitudes instead of establishing universal laws. He focuses on the personal aspect of this cosmopolitan ethic in terms of human relationships by inquiring into the obligations that we should have toward strangers. He begins by rejecting both a substantive universalism that would establish a unified value system for all of humanity[57] and the notion of a world government that would be the administrator of such a universalism,[58] arguing that cosmopolitanism cannot establish such a unified conception but rather must accept a diversity of attitudes about values and the practical implementation of values. At the same time, he also rejects the notion of a complete cultural relativism with regard to values, insisting that as a practical matter all humans agree on a basic set of moral norms that include prohibitions on murder, torture, and theft, even if there are a variety of ways of justifying these norms.[59] And even though there are big differences in how people justify their values, there is general agreement in the moral judgments they make in their daily lives. Therefore, Appiah opposes dogmatic universalism of the kind that one finds in the Islamic fundamentalism of al-Qaeda. Such "counter-cosmopolitanism," as he calls it, seeks to impose one uniform value system on the whole world, with violence if necessary. Such counter-cosmopolitans are often linked to or identical with the racists and chauvinists who seek to deny rights to a portion of humanity, suggesting that this portion is inherently inferior or unworthy.

Because he rejects the imposition of a single universal ideology upon the world yet at the same time recognizes that all people make similar moral judgments in their daily lives, Appiah argues for the development of specific relationships between strangers as the foundation of a cosmopolitan attitude: "Still, engagement with strangers is always going to be engagement with particular strangers; and the warmth that comes from shared identity will often be available."[60] The engagement with particular people is for him the basis of a practical cosmopolitanism in which the building of individual relationships between strangers is always possible in spite of disagreements and in which the warmth of such relationships, rather than their rationality, becomes the defining characteristic. By emphasizing the importance of specific, concrete relationships between individuals, he moves his discussion toward personal bonds: "But the great lesson of anthropology is that when the stranger is no longer imaginary, but real and present, sharing a human social life, you may like or dislike him, you may agree or disagree; but, if it is what you both want, you can make sense of each other in the end."[61] Appiah's argument for cosmopolitanism depends on the idea that when there is a specific connection between two people, they can overcome cultural differences in the negotiation of their relationship. Yet, the one condition here is that this is only possible when "it is what you both want." The development of a practical cosmopolitanism depends upon desire. Though Appiah develops explicitly the argument "that we have obligations to strangers,"[62] this argument depends on our desires, the fact that we would want to develop a relationship to a stranger. While his focus is on the practical implementation of a cosmopolitan ethic, he ends up appealing to willfulness and desire rather than duty in the relationship to strangers, thereby eventually broaching the theme of love, though only in an indirect way. Cosmopolitanism implies not just a particular morality but also a kind of love.

This underlying presumption of his argument, though only indicated fleetingly in his writing, is in actuality a major motivator of Appiah's cosmopolitanism. In developing a philosophical account of moral cosmopolitanism, he couches his argument within a narrative of his own upbringing as the child of a Ghanian father and an English mother.[63] His existence as the progeny of this cross-cultural marriage allows him to provide insights into cultural conflict and diversity that ultimately stem from a cosmopolitan love between his two parents. It is this love that makes the practical cosmopolitan relationships Appiah describes in the book possible.

Appiah's practical cosmopolitanism, driven by a *desire* to have relationships with strangers, leads to the argument for a cosmopolitan love. The defining feature of cosmopolitan love is that it emerges out of specific existing local relationships but struggles to break their limitations. This transgressing of such relationships becomes a form of liberation in that it reckons, proposes, and embraces new relationships. Family love is grounded in a heavy tension between a parental love that traps the children and children's struggling desire to turn away from the parents in order to form personal bonds with strangers. Similarly, romantic love does not follow a rational or preordained script but will transgress economic, cultural, and political boundaries not simply as a matter of a general principle of justice but as an intense desire to know and cherish an outsider regardless of ethnicity, nationality, and class. Because we want to develop out of these existing relationships based on love, the path to cosmopolitanism cannot lie in a rejection of such relationships or even in their suspension in favor of justice. Through literature we can examine the way in which cosmopolitanism arises out of the transformation of these relationships themselves. In this sense, cosmopolitan love is a utopian endeavor that does not so much establish a cosmopolitan utopia but maintains a longing for it in the way loves develop.

Because this approach to cosmopolitanism depends on existing personal relationships, it is necessary to begin not with an abstract morality or rules of justice but with the relationships in which people are already embedded. The path to cosmopolitanism must go through an existing tradition. In focusing on the literary works of Lawrence and Chang, it will be possible to gauge the way in which their cosmopolitanism develops out of their perspective on love in their respective traditions. As transnational migrants, both writers projected their cosmopolitan desires and provocations onto their literary works, adopting a similar approach to love by empowering it to become a cosmopolitan sensibility that, on the one hand, engages with existing relationships within their cultures but, on the other, can freely transcend boundaries and merge China and the West in the twentieth century. Pursuing liberation from a homogenizing secular culture through a shared framework of cosmopolitan love, they explored the ways in which love can intervene in, rather than be easily and passively subjugated by, the hegemonic local and global discourses of modernism. Though they start within their own cultural traditions, they arrive at the same vision of freedom by establishing a common trajectory of love in which it can move through different phases of maturity. This approach to cosmopolitanism is important because it creates a secular possibility for transcending boundaries by providing a personal, as opposed to an economic or political, framework of cosmopolitan sensibility, forming a revised understanding of the possibility of individual liberation from the oppressions of both traditional structures and global modernization.

The Methodology of Third Term Comparison

The comparison between Lawrence and Chang brings up methodological issues of the validity and methods of such a comparison between texts from such disparate cultures. When a text from one cultural tradition is taken up in another one, biases are inescapable because they are the symptoms of the process by which any text is received in terms of the receiver's preconceptions, and previous scholarship has focused on uncovering the distortions and misunderstandings that such biases engender.[64] Yet, these biases do not have to constitute a barrier to comparison, which depends upon the mediation that is essential to all cultural reception. "Mediation becomes visible as preconception or bias,"[65] and Saussy emphasizes "that we are always in the midst of mediation, that mediation is our authenticity—whoever 'we' may be."[66] But if mediation is necessary, we do not have to treat the process of mediation as a liability or a source of distortion. Rather, we can take control of the mediation process by consciously choosing a bias, which is to say a particular intention, to guide the analysis. This conscious intention defines the third term that motivates the comparison and offers it a direction. When it comes to the methodology of comparison, the question that needs to be addressed first is the purpose of comparison, which must be established before the task of "excavating and activating the historically specific set of relationalities across time and space."[67] The inherent intention of comparing determines what I call the "third term comparison" method, which establishes at the outset a purpose that enables the concentration on two texts from two very distinctive cultural contexts, reestablishing and reshaping relationships. The third term allows us to investigate a text in its relationship to its own tradition and then to compare those two relationships to each other.

In Chinese, the equivalent word for comparison is 比 (bi). This word has a number of different meanings depending on various historical and cultural contexts, and one of the early and important meanings of the word 比 in *Hanyu da cidian* 漢語大詞典, a detailed Chinese dictionary, is "to compare" (比较). For instance, 比 can be found in the *Rituals of Zhou* (*Zhouli* 周礼), "comparing large and small, judging coarse and fine, in order to reward and punish."[68] The phrase indicates that the punishment or reward one receives is based on an authority's judgment, which is made by comparison in terms of size and quality. Comparison, traced back to this origin, serves as a basic judgment method to determine good and bad, usefulness and uselessness to the state and society.

The purpose of comparison provides the key to establishing the framework for a comparative method. On the one hand, comparison can be driven by power and struggle, thereby creating opposing binaries: inferiority and superiority, dominance and suppression, violence and hegemony.

Such a competition exhausts all energies and resources in conflict, leaving no more alternatives but survival and compliance in such an antagonistic system. Any comparison, therefore, can be bound up with a reduction to power politics that either bolsters the preexisting order or usurps it to establish a new order that is more hegemonic than the replaced one. Comparison, with this purpose, will not escape the singular logic of power struggle and therefore inevitably predetermines its own future of rigidity and languidness. This also explains the reason comparison is being eliminated in today's postmodern criticism. On the other hand, the idea of judgment for 比 is a mode of settling a conflict, not with violent competition but through a comparison that focuses on a greater purpose that determines the comparative framework. It is this third element of purpose that must be the focus of our attention, compelling us to carefully choose this purposive basis of comparison in order to promote an alternative to a binary mode. The problematic features inherently embedded in comparison and its long-standing use regulated by the sociopolitical tradition need to be recognized and addressed before we start any specific comparative projects. The comparative methodology is never a pure method but a practice of its own intention.

Comparative methodology, therefore, offers a redemption when it can de-binarize the comparative subjects as well as de-integrate comparison from fixed notions and stale norms. Dismantling this rigid binary tendency in comparison, third term comparison as a heuristic tool can oppose antagonizing comparative objects by defining a common purpose, which can then provide the basis for revealing disparate connections yet also subtle differences in a relational comparative mode.[69] In this way, the relation between China and the West as the two major comparative subjects would no longer have to be framed as opposing binaries or as competing hegemonies but can be seen as relational and conversational. It is always problematic to set up a comparison in such a way that it would essentialize China or the West within a binary model that attempts to define China or the West as a fixed opposition. After all, such a fixed definition would lead to a hardening of opposing political stances and inclinations. With a new level of tension between China and the West, it is more urgent to return to the origin of comparison and ponder upon the bigger picture of a common purpose.

This purpose is not an international agreement that is reached through discussions and negotiations, not an internationally cooperative project to achieve global economic development, not transnational work to save the poor or stop war, not an environmental agreement to solve the urgent problems of global warming and resource depletion. Although these concrete and significant cosmopolitan projects alleviate national and regional conflicts through cooperation and shared interests, their temporary shared goals must still contend with the deeper divisions and tensions that can eventually stymie cooperation. A more foundational and necessary purpose, therefore, is called upon to set an enabling condition for relationality and dialogue. Without attempting to solve the sociopolitical problems, it critiques the dominant sociopolitical orders through the personal and the private. This purpose can trigger a new perspective to approach the two comparative entities in order to know the entities themselves. The two comparative objects, China and the West, in this sense, are beyond the traditional notions of themselves. They could be reduced to the very basic unit, a free body or will, an author who is deeply embedded in his or her own local culture but also transgressing boundaries with the purpose of remeasuring and redefining the world. This way, the notions of China and the West are emancipated from a geopolitical structure to become fluid, dynamic, and transforming. They stop defining each other through opposition but instead open up to overlapping and echoing tendencies.

Such an approach can provide the conceptual tools to establish a China-West purposive comparative paradigm that can explore both the connections and the disparities between China and the West. Eschewing a symmetrical comparison or the comparative mode that emphasizes one-sided or mutual influences, the third term comparison method moves beyond binary comparison in order to draw attention to the third element, the purposive basis of comparison, to create the framework for illuminating the disparate connections.

Comparison of modern love is particularly appropriate for modern texts because of increasing relations between cultures. A comparison of the work of Lawrence and Chang de-binarizes China and the West with cosmopolitan love as the purposive basis, tailoring a China-West parallel comparison mode to an analogical mode that can explore the heterogeneous connections between East and West. Eschewing a symmetrical comparison or the comparative mode that emphasizes one-party or mutual influences, third term comparison moves beyond the binary comparison to create more space for illuminating the disparate connections. Such connections are embodied in the authorial literary features, cultural connotations, and theoretical problems in local and global modernity.

Consequently, the third term comparative mode is the key to discovering the common project of cosmopolitan love in Lawrence and Chang, who practiced a new concept of cosmopolitanism as poetic selves as well as real selves. The comparison can help Western readers to understand Chang and help Chinese readers to comprehend Lawrence, thus serving as an effective intercultural means to better understand these two important national writers and the cultures that they represent.[70] Moreover, the comparison, by revealing an alternative trajectory, allows Western readers to better understand the significance of Lawrence's work and helps Chinese readers to gain insight into Chang's work. In this comparative project, cosmopolitan love serves not simply as a persistent literary theme of universal importance but as a nexus of links between things that were previously thought to be separate. Furthermore, charged with rich ideological and cultural energy, the idea of cosmopolitan love forms an alternative logic or rhetoric of modernism. It can expand from the private sphere into the public as an existential and sociopolitical quest that motivates the individual to reimagine local particularities and a unitary global idiom.

Yet, the methodological focus on connections and similar love forms does not downplay the complex and underlying differences of each writer's response toward their local cultures as well as their idiosyncratic literary aesthetics. The equally important insight readers can gain from the comparison stems from the rich details of the unique artistic forms encoded with different sociopolitical, cultural, aesthetic, and metaphysical meanings. Lawrence and Chang, equally courageous truth tellers, share Nietzsche's countercultural orientation against most of their contemporaries and offer us alternative modes of thinking about love, the interrelation between family and society, and, overall, the meaning of our existence in a dramatically changing world.

As a result, the point of the comparison is not simply to compare two concepts of love in different cultures or historical periods. Rather, the comparison carries two sets of relationships: the disparate connections between the two authors and the respective authorial responses toward their own times. The relationship to the other author illuminates each author's specific choices and their consequences in their specific cultural contexts. Without the comparison, the rebellion is a necessary action rather than a particular choice. By comparing an author's choices with those of another author in a comparable context, we can see the differences between local contexts within the same problem area as well as better understand authorial attempts to address the problem. Each author's rebellion becomes one possibility within a field of alternatives. Therefore, the comparison makes it possible to invoke the alternative trajectory of realities in each context. By comparing the tension between Chang and her historical time with the tension between Lawrence and his time, the comparison illuminates the two historical times as much as each author illuminates the other. The historical limitations Chang faces become more intelligible when compared with the different limitations Lawrence is confronted with, and vice versa. These differences in limitations lead to different strategies in the two authors' works. Though both attempt to focus on the personal aspect of love as the driver of a revised attitude toward social, economic, and political structures, each author pursues a distinctive approach to this project, and the comparison highlights the choices made by each author.

Comparison always needs to involve writers who are in opposition to their times. Such opposition to the times not only is always a characteristic of great writers but more importantly creates the possibility of comparison for some purpose. Such tension is what needs to be compared. In contrast, a comparison between Jane Austen and Ling Shuhua is plausibly workable and yet not sufficiently revealing because love and marriage represented by both writers complied with and bolstered the social orders of their times. A comparison without a tension merely generates a one-dimensional view even though the common theme of love is salient and comparable. Lawrence's and Chang's proposed solutions to their times may have differed if they ever proposed any concrete solutions. Yet, their reactions toward their times are common: an adamant attitude of critique toward their times through the focus on a cosmopolitan love that investigates personal relationships in a way that leads to a critique of existing structures. It is the tension between the author and the historical time that allows the personal love to intervene in the sociopolitical problems and to tightly connect two seemingly distinctive authors and their cultures. The point of the comparison is not merely to find commonalities but to compare the ways in which a common purpose produces different conflicts in the two contexts.

This project is an attempt to discover not only the links between the two writers but more importantly the disparate connections the two writers formulated between East and West. Lawrence's and Chang's intellectual and literary methods to approach the world echo with a comparative methodology based on intention: an unyielding refusal to be integrated socially and politically in order to transcend the hegemonic constraints of the local. This purpose of critiquing is practiced not only in their writing but also in their way of living in real life. Motivated by a cosmopolitan logic, they both cross national borders to further their engagement with the world. Writing as migrants, both writers were motivated by cosmopolitan visions to test the mutability of Englishness or Chineseness in their own writings.

The comparison between Lawrence and Chang breaks down the binary between China and the West by focusing on how their common purpose provides the conceptual tool for analyzing the relationships between different cultures, which are themselves changing. Here, the methodological focus on connections and similar love forms does not at all downplay the complex and underlying differences of each writer's response toward their local cultures as well as their idiosyncratic literary aesthetics. Though they both pursue a similar vision of love, the differences in cultural context mean that the common purpose expresses itself in different ways in each culture. Lawrence and Chang are both pointing to transformations in and beyond their writings. The comparison of the two authors leads to transformations in both contexts without setting up one as better or worse than the other.

The third term comparative mode begins with the definition of a purposive basis of comparison, in this case cosmopolitan love, which allows us to see how a particular vision of love develops in different ways in China and the West. Rather than focusing on fixed concepts, the analysis takes their common purpose as a way to understand the complicated processes of conceptual change and transformation in each culture. Therefore, this analysis can highlight the similarities and differences between the two traditions in a way that can lead to the development of a rich intercultural mediation as a basis for new relationships, which might replace rivalry or universality in a time of conflict and cultural imperialism. The two writers' cosmopolitan practices hold particular value for today's increasingly insulated and chauvinistic political climates in China, the United States, England, and Europe.

Four Forms of Love: Structure of the Book

In imagining how love breaks down preexisting orders and creates alternative utopian realities, both Chang and Lawrence outline a common framework in which love divides into four forms, each corresponding to different phases of an ideal subject's maturity: parental, sexual, adulterous, and transcendental. Inspired by C. S. Lewis's *Four Loves*, which interprets love in a Christian sense, I tease out different ways love transforms human relationships in such a way that the subject moves through these four separate phases in a process of maturation toward cosmopolitanism. In each phase the subject's search for love creates an engagement with the world that frees the subject from the limitations of existing constraints to transform the character of its relationships. Starting with a youthful passion for the parent, an individual steps out of family to maturely engage with the world by pursuing a freedom in love before and outside marriage, eventually seeking fulfillment in an eternal peace of love. Following the transforming sensibility of an individual, each transformation of love corresponds to a cosmopolitan strategy with which Chang and Lawrence could engage their local societies as well as the homogenizing secular world.

At each phase, the transformation of the subject begins as an incoherence in the present that can eventually be resolved into an event. As Lauren Berlant describes, "The present is perceived, at first, affectively: the present is what makes itself present to us before it becomes anything else, such as an orchestrated collective event or an epoch on which we can look back."[71] Before the present becomes an event, it can only be perceived as "simultaneous, incoherent narratives of what's going on and what seems possible and blocked in personal/collective life."[72] While Berlant describes an event as a passive process of perception, for Lawrence and Chang there is a willful aspect in which the transformation is not the result of an impersonal coalescence of an event. Instead, the transformation is the culmination of a conflict in which there is a decision that establishes the outlines of a new kind of relationship. On a personal level, the subject achieves the transformation toward a cosmopolitan love to the extent that its search for love reveals the incoherence of an existing situation and places it in a position to make a decision to resolve the incoherence into a new type of relationship. The moment of transformation is not just a perception but a decision that is an expression of freedom. The readings in each of the following chapters describe this shift from the incoherent affective moment to a new relationship in an act of freedom. The passage from affective situation to new possibility in treacherous and uncertain because it depends on decision and action. The result of the movement can be either a failed or a successful transformation. Lawrence's stories tend to result in the subject's achievement of a new possibility. By contrast, Chang's stories generally move from the incoherent, affective situation to the subject's realization of an inability to achieve the desired transformation.

The following chapters describe these different possibilities in each of the stages of transformation, starting with the destabilization of parent-child love that seeks to develop into romantic love in chapter 1. Chapter 2 reveals the affective moments that lead into a transformational sexual love, and chapter 3 focuses on the shift from marital to adulterous love. These transformations create visions of an emancipation from nationalism and modernization, and chapter 4 describes views of positive or negative utopian alternatives and the achievement of freedom in religious transcendence. The transformations that move the subject across these four dimensions of love are neither accidents nor coincidences. They are integral to a cosmopolitan process of proceeding actions that dissolve local cultural constraints in pursuit of alternative forms of relationships in the private and public dimensions.

Freud's idea of the Oedipus complex, which scientifically reduces the parent-child dynamic to an Oedipal structure that is held to be universal, belongs to the inevitable modernization and secularization process in which globalization equates with homogenization. In chapter 1, I question the homogenizing aspect of Freud's Oedipus complex by looking into the details of two stories of parent-child love written by Chang and Lawrence. Freud interprets the love between parents and children as always adhering to an Oedipus complex that originates from children's inner conflicts. Chang and Lawrence reverse the perspective by recognizing parents and the local culture as the main drivers of the problem. They see the problem as the weakening of the incest prohibition instead of the bursting forth of an Oedipal desire. I focus on parent-child love in *Sons and Lovers* (1913) and Chang's short story "Xin jing" 心經 ("The Heart Sutra") (1943) to show how the emancipation from the love between parent and child in both writers creates a liberation not only from the local but also from the hegemonic secular discourse of science, in this case the global spread of Freud's theory of the Oedipus complex. The Freudian idea of Oedipus and Electra complexes treats the problem of incest as a problem of an irrepressible desire. Lawrence's and Chang's stories retrieve the notion of love as an emancipatory force by indicating that the problem is not the love of children for parents. Rather, the respective problematic local cultures in China and England have led the parents to fail in their love for the children by selfishly relaxing their own enforcement of the incest prohibition and trapping their children. In chapter 1, the incest prohibition is revealed to be a form of love in which parents suppress their own selfish desires in order to enable the children to pursue sexual love outside the family and in relationships with strangers.

In chapter 2, sexual love embodies for both writers the authorial cosmopolitan desire to liberate themselves from insulated nationalisms and conventions after they both left their own homelands for the wider world, shortly after the twentieth-century world wars. To Lawrence, the new world after World War I is the primitive South, whereas Chang turns after World War II to the rising power of the United States. Chapter 2 probes beneath the discursive surface of sexual love in Lawrence's novella *The Virgin and the Gipsy* (written in 1926 but published in 1930) and Chang's short story "Se, jie" 色，戒 ("Lust, Caution") (written in the 1950s but published in 1978). Both stories feature a withdrawal of a female character from her country to find her own expression elsewhere. Both authors tell similar stories to emphasize the power of love as subversion against the fervent patriotisms and ethical conventions of their times. Both women fall for men whom they, according to the rules of their local societies, are not supposed to love. Whereas Lawrence portrays a primitive love between an Anglo-Saxon woman and a low-class gypsy, Chang subverts Chinese nationalism by prioritizing love over the larger political cause. In their narratives, sexual love, fully charged with social defiance, becomes a force to transcend national boundaries to offer a liberation from a unitary nation-state political identity.

This defiance can grow from a pure sexual impulse to a more complex desire that shakes the institutional norms and ethics of marriage. Adultery, as an unethical deed and immoral stance, can symbolically disturb social norms and the dominant order. Chapter 3 argues that the seemingly modern adulterous love in Lawrence's *Lady Chatterley's Lover* (1928) and Chang's "Jinsuo ji" 金鎖記 ("The Golden Cangue") (1943) is an antimodern relationship. Modern relationships are so suffused with alienation that only adultery can be a pure form of love. In *Lady Chatterley's Lover*, for instance, the aristocratic family relationships are based on money and rationality. By challenging those relationships, the adultery in the novel challenges the subordination of love to such rationality. Adulterous love surpasses, undermines, and destroys the existing order to set up an alternative basis for modern society. Although Lawrence was excluded by the Bloomsbury Circle in England and Chang was not part of the Crescent Circle and never compatible with the mainstream of the Chinese Modernist movement, both authors display radically modernist styles in their turn against a revolutionary modernization that values progress and advancement in their homelands. Both writers reverse the dominant logic of modernization by setting their stories in isolated spaces where time seems not to be moving forward. Aesthetically, Lawrence disrupts realist language by embodying his heroic fighting in mythical scenes and symbolic characters that counter cold intellectualism and mechanical industrialization. A poignant cross-class adulterous love blatantly betrays the orderliness that is based upon the modern spirit: rationality and progress in industrial England. In Chang's story, this adulterous impulse is suppressed and transformed into a slow and claustrophobic violence. The failed adultery gives away Chang's lack of trust in either premodern Chinese convention or Westernized social order, whose Euro-American historicity decides on what is modern and what is not in non-European cultures. Rather, she reveals a desolated modernity in the form of "de-cadenced contrast,"[73] an alternative to the dominant logic of optimistic, forward-looking modernization. This results in an aesthetics of desolation and temporal/spatial confinement, which can be interpreted as her strategy to respond to the revolutionary changes within as well as beyond modern China. The seemingly immoral love affairs in Lawrence and Chang surprisingly raise an ethical question about the progress-driven, forward-looking social evolution that had gained global momentum.

The first three chapters illustrate how Lawrence and Chang react toward the new beliefs (Freudianism, nationalism, modernization) with which modern societies attempted to replace the religious God. The last chapter demonstrates the ways in which Lawrence and Chang, in their later careers abroad, created an alternative language of divine love to render secular existence transcendentally meaningful. In chapter 4, the transcendental love in Lawrence's *Women in Love* (1920) and Chang's autobiographical novel, *Xiao tuanyuan* 小團圓 (*The Little Reunion*) (2009), transfers lovers to another mysterious dimension of utopia. If the first three chapters reveal their utopian alternative through fiction, the two autobiographies addressed in the last chapter explicitly and directly express a universal loss of faith as well as their personal attempts to break restrictions in their local cultural discourses. Lawrence attains his secular rebirth through primitive sexual union, while Chang's transcendence takes the form of a negative utopia.

Although claiming authorial nonchalance toward war and revolution, Lawrence and Chang wove their sociopolitical critiques into every page of their love stories. Starting with their own cultural traditions, both writers developed specific affinities by establishing a similar idea of love that escaped and challenged modern discourses in a global context. It is the convergence reached through love that extends this authorial comparison project beyond the usual models of comparative studies: parallel, influence, and circulation. Love serves not only as the subject but more importantly as an effective means to respond to local cultures and global modernization. In other words, this love returns cosmopolitan commitment to individuals, which becomes an alternative to an administered cosmopolitanism conventionally practiced by nations and corporations. Both writers situated love at center stage to link their story worlds to the real worlds, the interior to the exterior, the local to the cosmopolitan, and the temporary to the ultimate. Love, voluntary and spontaneous, emerges in the two writers as a practice of freedom that pushes the boundaries of love defined by both China and the West to form disparate connections between them. This book shows the way in which two seemingly incompatible writers, D. H. Lawrence and Eileen Chang, developed a common cosmopolitan project in which love can lay out a path from local hegemonic discourses to a cosmopolitan freedom.

ONE

Incest Prohibition and Cosmopolitanism

The idea of cosmopolitan love seems contradictory. Cosmopolitanism is a political project of creating citizens of the world, while love is primarily a private feeling. Yet, cosmopolitan and love are linked because cosmopolitanism is about building relationships and love defines the finest form of human relationship. As a result, cosmopolitan love can mean that cosmopolitan relationships are best established upon the basis of love. Unfortunately, it is impossible to establish cosmopolitanism simply by universally loving one another as global citizens. Bonds of love are specific and cannot be extended willy-nilly to all of humanity all at once. So, if cosmopolitanism is linked to love, it would have to be through the gradual mediation of our immediate private loves. Could there possibly be a way in which our private loves might be cosmopolitan? To answer this question, it is easier to start with the opposite. That is, what kind of love would not be cosmopolitan, closing off any relationship to something foreign and distant? Here, the answer is obvious: incestuous love, which rejects the foreign. If incest is anti-cosmopolitan, the incest prohibition is a fundamentally cosmopolitan rule. Thus, to imagine a cosmopolitan love, we should begin with analyzing the incest prohibition, understood as the command that we love a stranger.

The incest prohibition, as the only universally held human rule, defines human culture as fundamentally cross-cultural.[1] Yet the prohibition also embodies a basic contradiction between the local and the foreign in human existence. We have a natural inclination toward what we have known, but the survival of human culture requires that we abandon the familiar in order to find love elsewhere, thus forcing children to take the first step away from their own parents and the local culture that they embody. By compelling children to seek a mate elsewhere than within the confines of the familial, the incest prohibition links the local with the foreign, encouraging a cosmopolitan sensibility that is essential to the reproduction of human culture. Since the primary function of the incest prohibition is to enforce and demand strong connections to strangers, the defining function of the incest prohibition is the foundation of cosmopolitan love and cosmopolitanism itself.

The incest prohibition also provides the framework for all morality. By forcing us to subordinate our instinctual desires to the following of a general rule, the incest prohibition compels us to suppress our immediate sexual desires in order to pursue a long-term relationship. As a suppression of individual desires, the incest prohibition establishes morality and, with it, culture.[2] In so doing, it establishes an opposition between desire and love, in which love involves self-restraint. The incest prohibition is thus the requirement of every morality and of every true love. When the incest prohibition is too weak to control incestuous desire, the foundation of humanity is undermined and dismantled, leading to a regressive humanity and barrenness in physical and cultural reproduction.

However, the incest prohibition that compels children to love strangers does not mean a blanket rejection of the past and of the familiar. Every marriage brings two families together, and this process does not involve the negation of the familiar in favor of something global. Rather, marriage is the beginning of an interaction between two family traditions. Consequently, the approach to cosmopolitan love and the incest prohibition cannot involve a rejection of past traditions in favor of a new universal culture. The purpose of the incest prohibition is not just to reject the family and the past but to establish a link.

Analogously, to link the familial and the foreign, we need to engage a process of comparison. Because the incest prohibition is a moral rule and morality is a cultural phenomenon, our consideration of the incest prohibition must be based on comparison, especially between two very distinctive cultural systems like China and the West. A comparison opens up a critical perspective that can transcend itself by taking a position above the familiar in contrast with the foreign, thereby reaching a cosmopolitan vision. This vision is constructed not by establishing a universal culture but by comparing two traditions with each other. The methodology of cultural comparison and the incest prohibition are mutually linked.

Every culture has its incest prohibition, but each culture manages it in a different way. When one specific narrative of incest is mistaken for something universal, we risk losing sight of the structuring character of the incest prohibition as a moral rule that is fundamentally cultural. Unfortunately, our understanding of incest has been dominated by a school of thought that stems from the Freudian interpretation, which believes in the primacy of incestuous desire rather than of the incest prohibition.[3] Freud's Oedipus complex, which reduces incest to a universal structure of desire defined by a single narrative taken from an ancient Greek tragedy, belongs to a modernization and secularization process in which globalization means homogenization. By seeing all incest as a case of a natural childhood desire to sleep with the mother and kill the father, Freud's homogenizing scientific approach subsumes all incest within the Oedipus complex. By presuming that child psychology is everywhere the same, it takes this Oedipal psychology to be the single narrative of incest. This method thereby establishes an imperialist approach to incest by imposing a specific case as the universal. This method also mistakenly presumes the primacy of incestuous desire, thereby rejecting the idea that it is the incest prohibition that creates incestuous desire.[4]

My approach to cosmopolitanism, on the contrary, sheds light on local specificities by focusing on incest prohibition rather than incestuous desire, morality rather than instinct, love rather than desire. As we look at specific stories of incest, we find that parental culture, not infantile desire, is the basis of every example of incest. If this is the case, the problem of incest outlines a cultural problem that demands a comparison to understand.

Consequently, a consideration of the details of two stories of incest written by D. H. Lawrence and Eileen Chang can illuminate the specificities and variations in the structuring of incestuous desire and its prohibition that Freud overlooks. If Freud interprets incest as conforming to a universal Oedipal dynamic that originates from children, Chang and Lawrence reverse the perspective by recognizing parents and the local culture as the main drivers of incestuous desire. The critique of the transgressive love between parent and child in both writers leads to a liberation not only from the local but also from the hegemonic secular discourse of science, in this case, the global spread of Freudian theory.

Sons and Daughters in Love

Published in 1913, *Sons and Lovers* is Lawrence's semiautobiography. Like Lawrence himself, Paul Morel is born into a miner's family, a life filled with poverty, violence, and painful domestic quarrels. The problematic marital relation of Paul's parents directly leads to his mother's obsession with her sons and Paul's strong fixation on his own mother. This excessive mother-son love impedes Paul from developing any connection with other women when he reaches manhood.

Unable to escape his abnormal obsession with his mother, Paul enters into two destructive love relationships. The first is with Miriam, a girl he has known since he was a teenager. It is a highly spiritual and moral affair, very much like his relationship to his mother, Gertrude, which is also why Paul breaks off his relationship with Miriam. His second lover, Clara, is exclusively sensual and instinctual, but Paul fails to fall in love with her because he cannot reconcile his mind and body. The death of Gertrude finally releases Paul from his incestuous attraction to his mother and leaves him free to explore his own life at the end of the novel.

"The Heart Sutra," a short story published in 1943, represents a similar, even more transgressive, incestuous love. After her twentieth birthday, Xu Xiaohan 許小寒, the heroine, is anxious about losing the love of her father, Xu Fengyi 許峯儀. She emotionally attaches herself to Fengyi, excludes amorous relationships with boys, and even cruelly manipulates a sincere admirer to gain Fengyi's attention. She also despises, even spitefully challenges, her mother, an amiable, lovable, traditional housewife. Surprisingly, Xiaohan's problems are reciprocated by the father, since Fengyi desires his daughter. Paul's mother never threatens him sexually, but Fengyi has an affair with Xiaohan's friend Lingqing 綾卿, who looks like Xiaohan, to escape from this incestuous desire for his daughter. Here, the father's incestuous desire prevents him from properly loving his daughter.

In premodern China, the narrative of incest was usually shady and peripheral. The incestuous desire, as a cultural taboo, was generally situated as a subplot or evasive narrative in traditional Chinese literature. Andrew Plaks points out the noticeable and problematic "pseudo-incestuous" relation established by marriage rather than by blood in *Jin Ping Mei* 金瓶梅 (*The Golden Lotus*) and *Honglou meng* 紅樓夢 (*The Story of the Stone*).[5] In modern China, Cao Yu's play *Leiyu* 雷雨 (*The Thunderstorm*) exemplifies a sensationalist treatment of incest, which pushes the plot to a tragic climax. However, the incest in *The Thunderstorm* is still not a direct mother-son or father-daughter incestuous relation. The incestuous entanglements are still limited to pseudo-incestuous relationships by marriage.[6] "The Heart Sutra" therefore is the first Chinese story that strongly and directly reveals the incestuous desire between a daughter and her biological father.

Chang was the first writer who openly expressed the incestuous

impulse in semicolonial China, while Lawrence was the first who percep-
tively reflected upon the complex mother-son issue in modern England.
Lawrence and Chang, male and female, with a thirty-year time gap and
two distinctive cultural backgrounds, are so similar that the immediate
question would be whether Lawrence influenced Chang. Chang did read
some of Lawrence's works, according to her first husband, Hu Lancheng
胡蘭成, in his autobiography, *Jinsheng jinshi* 今生今世 (*This Life, These
Times*). Indeed, some of Lawrence's works were translated into Chinese as
early as the 1920s. A Chinese translation of Lawrence's short story "Two
Blue Birds" was published in 1929, and translations of *The Woman Who
Rode Away and Other Stories* and *Lady Chatterley's Lover* were published
in 1936.[7] Other modern Chinese writers, such as Yu Dafu 郁達夫 and Shen
Congwen 沈從文, admit that they were impressed by Lawrence's work.

The question is then whether Lawrence influenced Chang after she read
his stories and, if so, to what extent she was influenced. Hu Lancheng writes
that Chang "talked about literary works written by George Bernard Shaw,
Aldous Huxley, William Somerset Maugham, and D. H. Lawrence [. . .]
but their talents have limitations."[8] It is certain that Chang and Lawrence
shared the same interests and concerns in life. She may even have wanted to
build on Lawrence while addressing their shared topics. However, there is
no substantive evidence to quantify the degree to which Chang was directly
influenced by Lawrence. Instead, Freud's influence upon both Chang and
Lawrence is more salient and thereby worth examining.

Lawrence, Chang, and Freud

Freud's worldwide influence pervaded and permeated the culture of the
twentieth century. As the most influential psychologist in the twentieth
century, Freud provided the world with his pioneering psychological theories. In such scholarly works as *The Interpretation of Dreams* (1900), *A
Case of Hysteria* (1901–5), *Three Essays on Sexuality* (1901–5), and *Beyond
the Pleasure Principle* (1920–22), Freud analyzes the power of sexuality
in the unconscious. For Freud, the sexual drive in humans determines
their personalities and behaviors. His emphasis on the sexual motivation ingrained in the unconscious overturned reason's central position in
motivating human behavior. He suggests that the Oedipus complex might
have always existed in human history but had never been named until he
did so.

Freudian theory definitely offers a convenient reading of the transgressive youths Paul Morel and Xu Xiaohan, given certain features of the Oedipus complex in the two stories. In *The Interpretation of Dreams*, Freud wrote about the parental fixation by analyzing the literary works *Oedipus Rex* and *Hamlet*. He first used the term "Oedipus complex" in 1910 (the year Lawrence's mother died and during which Lawrence was writing *Paul Morel*, an early version of *Sons and Lovers*) when he published the article "A Special Type of Choice of Object Made by Men." In this article, Freud claims that a son "begins to desire his mother herself in the sense with which he has recently become acquainted, and to hate his father anew as a rival who stands in the way of this wish he comes, as we say, under the dominance of the Oedipus complex."[9] Also, in his 1912 paper "On the Universal Tendency to Debasement in the Sphere of Love," Freud offers two libidinal currents, the "affectionate" and the "sensual." The affectionate current emerges in the period of infancy and carries "components of erotic interest" toward the mother and hostility toward the father. The sensual current will join the affectionate current and retreat (due to social barriers) but is fixated on the first "object-choices."[10]

It is easy to identify the kinship between Lawrence's *Sons and Lovers* and Chang's "The Heart Sutra" with the family romances Freud describes. Paul Morel in *Sons and Lovers* and Xiaohan in "The Heart Sutra" both illustrate some symptoms of Freud's Oedipus complex. The protagonists, postponing their own maturation, share an intimate bond of affection with the opposite-sex parents and hold hostility toward the same-sex parents. Freud argues that such parent-child incest arises out of the inner psychology of the child, whose sexual desire for the opposite-sex parent is frustrated by the presence of the same-sex parent.

Both Paul and Xiaohan resist growing up because they are anxious about their detachment and separation from the opposite-sex parents. At the age of twenty-three, Paul still feels that "the deepest of his love belonged to his mother. When he felt he had hurt her, or wounded his love for her, he could not bear it."[11] Even after having Miriam as his girlfriend, Paul still behaves capriciously like a child. On the day when Paul wants to break up with Miriam, she "bent her head, pondering. He was an unreasonable child. He was like an infant which, when it has drunk its fill, throws away and smashes the cup. [. . .] She cried: 'I have said you were only fourteen—you are only *four*!'" (340). Even though he was struggling to dislodge his mother from his sweethearts, Paul unconsciously stays as a child so that he will not leave Gertrude. His claim that he will not marry anyone illustrates Paul's deep attachment to his mother.

The same claim is made by Xiaohan in front of her father. "She pulled at his sleeve and tried to slip her hand inside the cuff. She said quietly: 'I'll never leave you as long as I live.'"[12] Her father understands why she intentionally resists becoming an independent grown-up. Fengyi declares, "'I know why you don't want to ever grow up.' [. . .] 'You're afraid that if you grow up, we wouldn't be as close anymore, right?'"[13] "By the postponing of sexual maturation," according to Freud in *Three Essays on Sexuality*, where he examines the incest barrier, "time has been gained in which the child can erect, among other restraints on sexuality, the barrier against incest, and can thus take up into himself the moral precepts which expressly exclude from his object-choice, as being blood-relations, the persons whom he has loved in his childhood."[14] According to the Freudian interpretation, Paul and Xiaohan both suspend their own growth, but this delay of sexual maturation in fact allows them to extend the time of their incestuous relationships with their parents.

According to this interpretation, the incestuous love Paul and Xiaohan both embrace compels them to hate their same-sex parents as rivals and simultaneously to resist heterosexual relations outside the family. Paul defends his mother with utmost love and resents his father, Walter, especially when Walter, drunk and violent, beats Gertrude. Lawrence writes, "Paul hated his father. As a boy, he had a fervent private religion. 'Make him stop drinking,' he prayed every night. 'Lord, let my father die,' he prayed very often" (85). He hates his father deeply not merely because he is drunk and violent but also because Paul unconsciously regards his father as his rival in winning Gertrude's love.

Xiaohan also distances herself from her mother because the closeness to the mother repulses and frightens her. When she shares a rickshaw with her mother on a rainy day, "her leg pressed firmly against her mother's— her own flesh and blood! She suddenly felt a gush of intense disgust and terror. Who did she fear? Whom did she hate? Her mother? Herself? They were simply two women in love with the same man. She detested her own muscles and the warm muscles which were firmly pressed against her. Ah, her own mother."[15] Xiaohan's unspeakable disgust and terror toward her mother are rooted in her jealousy and hostility toward the woman who also loves Fengyi. Both Paul and Xiaohan regard their same-sex parents as their love rivals.

An incestuous passion also prevents the youths from bonding with others. Paul is unable to maintain his relationship with Miriam, his spiritual lover, as well as Clara, a sexual woman, because of his absolute love for Gertrude. When Gertrude and Paul discuss the women he wants to marry, Paul laments to his mother, "I never shall meet the right woman while you live" (395). Paul's relationships with Miriam and Clara are merely counterfeit, unable to offer the satisfaction and fulfillment Gertrude provides.[16] Likewise, cruelly refusing and rejecting all the boys who love her, Xiaohan cannot love anyone else except her own father. Resolving not to marry, she has desperately maintained the father-daughter love since she was seven. It consequently has been common to approach both *Sons and Lovers* and "The Heart Sutra" from the perspective of the Freudian Oedipus complex. Critics, starting from Alfred Kuttner, Daniel Weiss, Frederick Hoffman, and Shirley Panken, have investigated Lawrence's *Sons and Lovers* in light of Freudian theory.[17] Kuttner's essay, the earliest well-acknowledged interpretation, uses Freud's theory to analyze *Sons and Lovers*,[18] and Geoffrey Harvey, for example, notes of the novel:

> *Avant garde* intellectuals, prompted by professional psychoanalysts, who took a keen interest in this novel, drew attention to a very different interpretation inspired by the psychoanalysis of Sigmund Freud—then very much in vogue—that the intense mutual love of mother and son is abnormal and essentially destructive, a view which still dominates critical discussion of the novel.[19]

Intellectuals regard *Sons and Lovers* as a literary representation of Freud's Oedipus complex first because Lawrence himself offered a Freudian split theory of his novel in a letter to Edward Garnett.[20] Second, Lawrence changed the title from *Paul Morel* to *Sons and Lovers*, which foregrounds Freud's triangle, mother-son-sweetheart relationship and downplays other matters, such as Paul's complicated personality.[21]

As for Chang, there is no direct evidence showing that she read Freud's articles or books. Nevertheless, it is certain that she was exposed to Freud's psychoanalysis. The interest in sexuality and Freudian theory serves as a marker of modernism in the reason when subjectivity and psychology received unprecedented attention in China. Wendy Larson observes: "Along with the attack on the extended family, arranged marriage, and Confucian values in general, the Freudian centering of sexual desire became one perspective from which to dismantle the past and imagine a new future."[22] Chinese reception of Freudian sexual desire either sub-limated it to a sociopolitical cause or simply rejected it. As Larson notes:

> Although the prospects tendered in Freud's deeply sexual modern person were taken seriously and considered, disagreements, recognized or unrecognized, with some of the basic tenets of Freud's thought prevented Chinese writers from fully realizing the promise inherent in his work. Failing to appear are fictional characters like those of D. H. Lawrence, who are saturated with sexual desire and derive almost every imaginable meaning from that desire.[23]

Although Chang does not dwell on sexuality as explicitly as Lawrence, Larson believes that she "shows the most serious engagement with Freudian ideas" before Freud fever broke out in the 1970s and 1980s.[24]

Accordingly, although widely exposed to Freud's theories, China both assimilated and transformed Freud's ideas. The primary reason why Larson believes in Chang's more serious engagement with Freud is Chang's focus on the inner lives of women and sophisticated love relations. Yet, this very interest in women and love, which easily reminds us of Freud, cannot sufficiently prove Freud's direct influence. It could have been a shrewd strategy to win the Shanghai market, which boasted a large body of middle-class, educated women who were interested in women's subjectivity and romance. It also could have been the literary interest of Chang herself, an educated young woman who wanted to explore this very subject. The culture was infused with a strong sense of Freudian psychoanalysis and served as an agreeable social and literary climate for Chang to write about women's interior subjectivity. The Freudian influence, however, is neither direct nor extensive, as in Lawrence's case.

Cosmopolitan Revision of the Oedipus Complex: A Local Heterosexual Problem

Though Lawrence and Chang may have been triggered or slightly influenced by Freud's theory, they did not reduce incest to the inevitable desires of the child as the scientist Freud did. Rather, they decipher parent-child incestuous love as a local cultural problem that can serve as their starting point to seek a liberation from their respective societies as well as from a globalized scientific discourse.

Lawrence himself was the first to publicly reject the Freudian approach to his novel. After reading Alfred Kuttner's article "*Sons and Lovers*: A Freudian Appreciation," Lawrence took offense: "I hated the *Psychoanalysis Review* of *Sons and Lovers*. [. . .] My poor book: it was, as art, a fairly complete truth: so they carve a half lie out of it, and say 'Voila.' Swine!"[25] Lawrence's repudiation of Freud results primarily from their completely distinctive concepts about the unconscious, sexuality, idealism, and science. Lawrence started writing *Sons and Lovers* in 1910 when Freud, for the first time, offered the term "Oedipus complex" to describe a universal structure of desire that he first outlines in his *Interpretation of Dreams*. Lawrence and Freud very likely began their investigations at the same time but set up two distinctive analyses about the same tabooed subject. Frederick Hoffman also senses that *Sons and Lovers* was "only superficially affected" by Freud.[26] Mark Spilka shares the same observation: "Lawrence may well have written the book, at first, in accord with his own developing psychology, and then rewritten it in garbled accord with Freud's. . . . The novel takes its strength from Lawrence's psychology and its weakness (inadvertently) from Freud's."[27] The ostensibly conspicuous Freudian account conceals Lawrence's idiosyncratic interpretation of incestuous desire in the novel.

Lawrence's two books on the unconscious (*Psychoanalysis and the Unconscious* and *Fantasia of the Unconscious*) differ from Freud although they both address the same subject.[28] Anne Fernihough tries to answer the question of why Lawrence declares his hostility toward Freud despite their shared interest in the unconscious. She posits, "As Lawrence sees it, Freud's mistake is that he attempts to approach the unconscious through a scientific discourse . . . in that he attempts to systematize the one area of the psyche (the unconscious) which has hitherto been immune to, or capable of subverting system."[29] In other words, Lawrence rejects Freud's scientific approach, which misinterprets, standardizes, and censors the unconscious. For Lawrence, humans are noble and complex creatures with sympathy and emotion rather than lab rats with animal instinct and sexual drive. Rejecting Freud's aforementioned affectionate and sensual currents, Lawrence explains parent-child love as a result of excessive parental attention to the child's "sympathetic centres," an absolutely spiritual or emotional response, untainted by sexuality, which sparks the "voluntary centres."[30]

In "Parent Love," an essay in *Fantasia and the Unconsciousness*, Lawrence posits that abnormal parent-child love is rooted in an unhealthy husband-wife relationship. In this essay, Lawrence also provides a detailed and reliable analysis of how failed marriages push women to devour their sons: "A woman reaches her fulfillment through love, deep sensual love, and exquisite sensitive communion." She will not "break off to ask for more excitement" if the husband "undertake[s] the responsibility" and "give[s] himself perfectly to some further purpose [. . .] till he takes upon himself the silence and central appeasedness of maturity." However, if the husband fails to shoulder the responsibility to acquire maturity, the "love-craving" will drive the wife into "frenzy and disaster." The result is that the wife seeks "fulfillment in the deep passional self; diseased with self-consciousness and sex in the head, foiled by the very loving weakness of the husband who has not the courage to withdraw into his own stillness and singleness, and put the wife under the spell of his satisfaction, seeking whom she may devour."[31]

Consequently, the wife will shift her need for love to her children, leading to an extreme intensity of incestuous desire between mother and son that disturbs and deranges the son's "sympathetic-voluntary system" and leads to his frustration, even perversion.[32] Accordingly, Lawrence is aware of the flaws in heterosexual relations in British society. The husband's failure to carry out his responsibility and the wife's unsatisfied need for love both lead to the son's inability to love normally.

In *Sons and Lovers*, Lawrence illustrates how the husband's alcoholism, violence, immaturity, and irresponsibility compel the wife's love to shift toward her sons and eventually Paul's excessive attachment to the mother. Different from Freud, who blames incestuous desire on the child's Oedipus complex, Lawrence details the experience of an incestuous desire resulting from a dysfunctional family and the weakening of the incest prohibition on the part of the parents. Lawrence thereby culturally contextualizes the situation of incest.

Walter Morel drinks and bullies the family, especially his wife, Gertrude. His irresponsibility makes the whole family miserable. One night, after drinking, Morel and Gertrude have a fight. "He came up to her, his red face, with its blood-shot eyes, thrust forward, and gripped her arms. She cried in fear of him, struggled to be free. Coming slightly to himself, panting, he pushed her roughly to the outer door, and thrust her forth, slotting the bolt behind her with a bang" (33). Gertrude is forced by Morel out of doors on a cold night. Morel resorts to alcohol to escape from his family responsibility. When he is in a pub, "he was glad. In a minute or two, they had thawed all responsibility out of him, all shame, all trouble, and he was clear as a bell, for a jolly night" (57). Gertrude's love for her husband fades, and she breaks the attachment with him. After Paul was born, "her self no longer set towards him [the husband], helplessly, but was like a tide that scarcely rose, standing off from him. After this she scarcely desired him. [. . .] she did not mind so much what he did, could leave him alone" (62). Morel also senses his wife's change. "His wife was casting him off, half regretfully, but relentlessly; casting him off and turning now for love and life to the children" (62). The broken marriage results in the mother's excessive love for her sons, which leads eventually to Paul's inability to love other women.

A Freudian reading does not recognize these specific family dynamics as the source of parent-child incestuous desire. Rather, he interprets such desire as part of an inevitable and universal development within the psyche of the child that follows the Oedipal story of incestuous desire for the mother and the wish to kill the father. He thereby reduces literary works to the globalized dominance of science, thus oversimplifying organic, lived experiences and undermining the importance of local cultural details. Lawrence vehemently repudiated Freud's theory, while Chang wrote the story "The Heart Sutra" with more of the traditional filial love than with Freud in her mind. Lawrence and Chang differ from the scientist Freud in that they focus on local cultural dynamics as well as organic lived experience. Also, the mutual love between parent and child in both writers, potentially led by the parent, further defies the rigid definition of the one-way Oedipus/Electra complex that originates from the child's desire, thereby indicating that Lawrence and Chang actually provided an alternative understanding of this transgressive love.

As demonstrated, Gertrude was the source because she fed on Paul's obsession for her. The incestuous love is mutual rather than merely a son's problem in Freud's sense. Paul and his mother love each other as intensely as lovers do. When Gertrude is ill, Paul sits by her bed:

> "Doesn't it [Gertrude's hair] tickle you?" he said, gently putting it back. "It does," she replied. His face was near hers. Her blue eyes smiled straight into his, like a girl's, warm, laughing with tender love. It made him pant, with terror, agony and love (139)

The excessive mutual intimacy is more evident when they have an argument about Paul's girlfriend, Miriam. Gertrude cries with tears:

"I can't bear it. I could let another woman—but not her—she'd leave me no room, not a bit of room—"

And immediately he hated Miriam bitterly.

"And I've never—you know, Paul—I've never had a husband—not really—"

He stroked his mother's hair, and his mouth was on her throat.

"And she exults so in taking you from me—she's not like ordinary girls."

"Well, I don't love her, mother," he murmured, bowing his head and hiding his eyes on her shoulder in misery. His mother kissed him a long, fervent kiss:

"My boy!" she said, in a voice trembling with passionate love. (252)

Gertrude is in despair because Miriam substitutes herself as Paul's spiritual love. Considering his mother as the supreme love of his life, Paul cannot establish a romantic attachment to any other woman. He strokes his mother's hair while "his mouth was on her throat." She loves him back with "a long, fervent kiss." Their mutual passion suggests something more than an Oedipus complex in Paul; rather, they reveal their profound love for each other like devoted lovers. The mother initiates and always leads this relation.

It is his deep fixation on the mother that yields Paul's detachment from other girls, which further flaws his heterosexual relations. The upper center—mind, emotion, and spirituality—is more valued and emphasized than the lower center—the body. The mother's fanatical love for her son enables the upper sympathy to be "abnormally, inflamedly excited," as Lawrence observes in the aforementioned essay "Parent Love."[33] Lawrence excludes the possibility of sensual incest but posits that this strong connection between mother and son is a spiritual, sacred love. In the same essay, Lawrence continues:

All your tenderness, your cherishing will not excuse you. It only deepens your guilt. You have established between your child and yourself the bond of further sympathy. I do not speak of sex. I speak of pure sympathy, sacred love. The parents establish between themselves and their child the bond of the higher love, the further spiritual love, the sympathy of the adult soul.[34]

The young man is unable to set up a healthy heterosexual relationship with his girlfriend or wife because of the long-standing spiritual love established with his own mother. He can neither emancipate himself from this formidable spiritual love to create a new bond nor love a girl he is physically attracted to. He separates spiritual love from physical love and cannot harmonize both because of the mother.

Paul fails to obtain fulfillment from either the extremely spiritual Miriam or the highly sexual Clara, both of whom fail to take over the mother's place. Paul tells Miriam, "I have given it [a spiritual love] to you this long, long time; but not embodied passion. See, you are a nun. I have given you what I would give a holy nun—as a mystic monk to a mystic nun" (292). As "his conscience, not his mate," Miriam is cast away for Clara, from whom Paul can feel warmth and passion (337). Paul fails to establish a pleasurable connection with Miriam because he is unable to reconcile physical and spiritual love, of which the latter has already been exhausted by the mother. Lawrence describes Paul's dilemma and confusion when he and Miriam live together for a week. He "wore her out with his passion before it was gone. He had always, almost willfully, to put her out of count, and act from the brute strength of his own feelings. And he could not do it very often, and there remained afterwards always the sense of failure and of death. If he were really with her, he had to put aside himself and his desire. If he would have her, he had to put her aside" (334).

After leaving the highly spiritual Miriam, Paul turns to another extreme by indulging himself in the instinctual, sexual Clara: "When he started love-making, the emotion was strong enough to carry with it everything, reason, soul, blood, in a great sweep. [. . .] Gradually the little criticisms, the little sensations were lost, thought also went, everything borne along in one flood. He became, not a man with a mind, but a great instinct" (408). The blood, a symbol for instinctive desire, is supremely dominant. However, his impersonal passion for Clara is not love but desire. When Paul is with Clara, he reflects, "Clara was not there for him, only a woman, warm, something he loved and almost worshipped, there in the dark. But it was not Clara. And she submitted to him. The naked hunger and inevitability of his loving her, something strong and blind and ruthless in its primitiveness, made the hour almost terrible to her" (398). It is natural to resort to pure sex in which the spiritual mother is absent and silenced, regardless of its destructiveness and debasement. Paul is unable to love any of his sweethearts because of his profound and unspeakable love for Gertrude, the first love he is faithful to throughout his life.

The spiritual love for his mother hinders the son's fulfillment and leaves him nothing but suffering, despair, perversion, and emptiness. As Lawrence asserts in another essay, "The Incest Motive and Idealism":

> [The man] recognizes the fact that his emotional, even passional, regard for his mother is deeper than it ever could be for a wife. This makes him unhappy, for he knows that passional communion is not complete unless it be also sexual. He has a body of sexual passion which he cannot transfer to a wife. He has a profound love for his mother. Shut in between walls of tortured and increasing passion, he must find some escape or fall down the pit of insanity and death. What is the only possible escape? To seek in the arms of the mother the refuge which offers nowhere else. And so the incest-motive is born.[35]

In *Sons and Lovers*, Paul knows that "the deepest of his love belonged to his mother" (255). He also claims to his mother, "I never shall meet the right woman while you live" (395). No one can replace his mother, who supports his life and faces the world with him. The tie with his mother is "the strongest tie in his life. When he thought around, Miriam shrank away. There was a vague, unreal feel about her. And nobody else mattered" (261).

For Paul, his mother is the only person in this world that matters and stays real. "There was one place in the world that stood solid and did not melt into unreality: the place where his mother was. Everybody else could grow shadowy, almost non-existent to him, but she could not. It was as if the pivot and pole of his life, from which he could not escape, was his mother" (261). This unrivaled love will haunt the man and impede the fulfillment that a grown-up individual should achieve. His marriage will be poisonous and disastrous to himself, his wife, and his children. The happiness that marriage brings to the man will not outweigh the parental love that is lost. Lawrence observes in "Parent Love," "Each one begins to fret for the beauty of the lost, non-sexual, partial relationship. The sexual part of marriage has proved so—so empty. [. . .] The best is missing. The rest isn't worth much."[36] The longing for the irreplaceable love of the mother is the origin and the driver of the son's incestuous love. This vicious cycle of destruction will pass from generation to generation. As Lawrence claims in "Parent Love," "There is either a family of children whom the dissatisfied parents can devote themselves to, thereby perverting the miserable little creatures: or else there is divorce. [. . .] There has been no vital inter-change at all in the whole of this beautiful marriage affair."[37]

Although it seems that *Sons and Lovers* revolves around Paul's psy-chological growth and dilemma, the trajectory of his life is actually deter-mined by the mother. The reasons behind the abnormal mother-son love go beyond the Oedipus complex and the incestuous motivation Freud claims. Focusing on parents rather than children, Lawrence reverses Freud's psychologically generic reading of parent-child incestuous love by revealing such issues as frustrated marriage and unhealthy heterosexual relations in a broader cultural milieu. If the problem of incestuous love resides in parents rather than in children, as Lawrence reveals, his radi-cal reading of the transgressive parent-child love allegorically questions the normative narrative of England's local culture. Therefore, the parent-child love, unfit as a social norm, realistically reflects complicated domes-tic dynamics and symbolically deconstructs the long-lasting, problematic aspects of English culture.

Distorted Filial Piety in the Cultural Unconscious

Lawrence's observation illustrates the problems of heterosexual relations embedded in Western modern culture, while Chang's depiction of the incestuous desire between a Chinese daughter and her father exposes how the weakening of the incest prohibition is disguised by a traditional Chinese morality of filial piety. The Freudian Oedipus complex does not influence a colonized writer to the extent that Franco Moretti presumes in his notion of "wave."[38] Rather, it merely triggered and found affinities with China's unconsciousness.

A year earlier than "The Heart Sutra," Chang wrote an essay, "Demons and Fairies," in which she points out the profound link between suppressed passion and filial piety in traditional Chinese culture. She writes: "The preoccupation with parental remains can be explained by the abnormal development of filial sentimentality in China. The Chinese demand that filial affection be a grand consuming passion, and since it is the only legiti-mate passion it achieves heroic proportions."[39] Chang believes that filial piety has abnormally developed into a kind of sentimentality equal to lov-ers' passion. She continues in this essay, "A study of the behavior of model sons who, with the fervor of cannibalistic self-sacrifice, cut pieces of flesh from their thighs to make a medicinal soup for sick parents, shows them to be people madly in love."[40] There is a close link between the abnormal passion and filial affection, but Chinese Confucians justified this abnormal and distorted passion between parents and children as a grand and heroic virtue. "The Heart Sutra," therefore, is Chang's continued fictional exploration of this distorted passion in the guise of filial piety (*xiao* 孝).

Filial piety is one of the four major virtues highly valued by Confucian society and practiced in every Chinese person's lived experience.[41] Numerous pieces of classical Chinese literature praise this noble merit, and one can easily provide some quick examples. A modern reader may sense something peculiar about the extreme passion of filial piety in the classical folk stories. For instance, in the Han dynasty, a girl named Cao Er 曹娥 drowned after jumping into the river to retrieve her father's dead body. This real story was recorded in classical literature, and we can easily draw its connection to Chang's comment about the Chinese obsession with "parental remains." Cao Er has been respected as the most filial daughter; however, if we follow Chang's logic and read Cao Er from a totally different perspective, the daughter's incomprehensible attachment to her father is tantamount to a lover's passion. This passion reminds us of numerous love tragedies in traditional Chinese texts, such as *Liang shanbo yu zhu yingtai* 梁山伯與祝英台 (*The Butterfly Lovers*) and *Honglou meng* 紅樓夢 (*The Story of the Stone*), in which the young hero or heroine dies of heartbreak due to the separation from the lover.

In "Kongque dongnan fei" 孔雀東南飛 ("The Peacock Southeast Flew"), a Yuefu poem of the third century AD, the mother's irrational obsession with her son forces the son to divorce his beloved wife. It has been a lasting tradition in Chinese culture for sons to have a deep piety toward their mothers while the mothers hold grudges and are jealous toward the daughters-in-law. Ming Dong Gu calls this Chinese version of the Oedipus complex a "muted complex," which Chinese writers were unable to express overtly in literature. Gu asserts, "In a muted oedipal situation, the oedipal relationship may be a conflict between father and son; a triangular conflict involving mother, son, and son's wife; a son's insatiable longing for maternal love; a daughter's incomprehensible inhibition against love and marriage; or a male person's erotic love for an aunt, or mother's sister, stepmother, or even mother's close maid."[42] Gu contends that these phenomena, covertly existing in traditional Chinese families, indicate the hidden passion between mother and son, father and daughter. Yet, this distorted passion is not simply an example of the Freudian Oedipus complex because these phenomena are framed by a Chinese cultural unconsciousness. It risks oversimplification by conveniently borrowing Freud's term to explain this Chinese phenomenon. The incomprehensible passion for the opposite-sex parents existed in classical Chinese literature but had been muted and misinterpreted as merely filial piety. As the only outlet Chinese people have to release their surplus passion, the excessive affection between parent and child actually covers and hides an eccentric passion. One can easily find evidence of the structure of this incestuous desire in "The Heart Sutra."

While sitting on a sofa alone on her twentieth birthday, Xiaohan and Fengyi fancy that they can be lovers. The blood relation, however, forbids such desire and arouses guilt at their thoughts of incest.

> He, after all, would still be her father, and she, after all, would still be his daughter, even if he hadn't a wife, and even if she had another surname. The two of them subconsciously shifted towards the opposite ends of the sofa at the same time and sat a little farther apart. Both felt a little ashamed.

> 他究竟還是她的父親，她究竟還是他的女兒，即使他沒有妻，即使她姓了另外一個姓，他們兩人同時下意識地向沙發的兩頭移了一移，坐遠了一點。兩人都有點羞慚。[43]

Xiaohan's feeling toward the father is more like a lover's or a wife's. The passionate daughter could very easily be recognized as the source of the transgressive father-daughter love, and Paola Zamperini reads the story accordingly primarily in terms of "Xiaohan's demonic desire."[44] Xiaohan refuses to grow up in order to stay close with her father. When her friend Lingqing asks Xiaohan facetiously: "Are you planning on being a child all your life?" Xiaohan responds, "Even if I did, what of it? It's not as if no one in my family would put up with it!"[45] Xiaohan is determined to stay with her parents forever, which reminds us of the aforementioned filial excess. She would gently slide "her forefinger up and down along his [her father's] nose."[46] When she finds her father having an affair with Lingqing, Xiaohan is exasperated like a jealous wife and tries desperately to destroy this love affair.

However, the salient feature of the filial passion from a daughter is actually derived from her father's incestuous desire. When Xiaohan explicitly shows that no one in her family would be able to stop her from playing the child and staying forever with the parents, it indicates a sign of weakened moral prohibition in her family. Later, Fengyi secretly has an affair with Lingqing, who is the same age and has the same looks as Xiaohan. Lingqing as the surrogate fulfills Fengyi's incestuous desire for Xiaohan.

Tracing the origin of this passion, one discovers that Xiaohan's love starts with a genuine filial attachment in her childhood. When Fengyi attempts to explain how this love begins, he says, "I don't know how things got started. Seven or eight years already—when you were only that tall . . . before I knew it. . . . Ah, seven or eight years ago . . . that was the most cherished time, the golden period of love from parents, with no jealousy, prying, or suspicion."[47] Xiaohan's affectionate filial bond to the father burgeons in childhood but grows to an excessive passion, irrational and unconstrained.

Holding a stronger passion than Paul's mother, Fengyi loves Xiaohan as his daughter in the beginning, but this love is overtaken by an incestuous desire that he fails to prohibit in himself. One day, when Xiaohan is standing outside the window, Fengyi is gazing upon her through the glass:

> Through the glass, Fengyi's hand pressed against Xiaohan's arm—an ivory, round arm. Her robe was a beautiful flower-patterned gauze trimmed in red lacquer, on which the blue heads and fair faces of children were printed. The numerous children wriggled between his fingers. Xiaohan—that big, lovable child with lustrous beauty, a big, ivory fleshed child. . . . Fengyi withdrew his hand violently, as if he were burned by fire. His face changed color, and he turned around so as not to look at her.

> 隔著玻璃，峯儀的手按在小寒的胳膊上——象牙黃的圓圓的手臂，袍子是幻麗的花洋紗，硃漆似的紅底子，上面印著青頭白臉的孩子，無數的孩子在他的指頭縫裏蠕動。小寒——那可愛的大孩子，有著豐澤的、象牙黃的肉體的大孩子 . . . . . . 峯儀猛力掣回他的手，彷彿給火燙了一下，臉色都變了，掉過身去，不看她。[48]

This filial affection grows from childhood, year by year, to a transgressive passion and eventually turns drastically into a disastrous desire. As in Paul's case with his mother, the mutual love between father and daughter in Chang's story goes far beyond the one-way incestuous desire of the daughter for the father predicted by Freudian psychoanalytic theory. The father starts his parental love in the beginning, but it is gradually replaced by an incestuous desire that strongly influences the daughter, who cannot find a way to channel her passion except through the idea of filial love and is thus unable to focus on a love outside of the family. Even when Fengyi is gone, Xiaohan cannot develop a relationship with a man but rather stays under the influence of her mother. Since the incestuous situation results not from the daughter's desire but from the father's, the primary problem in the story is a moral one, in which the father succumbs to his desires and consequently fails to enforce the incest prohibition.[49] Its deterioration does not arise from the child's desire but from the failure of the parents to enforce this prohibition upon themselves in order to allow the children to be able to develop a love outside the family. The deterioration of the incest prohibition is hidden by the focus on filial sentimentality.

Chang seriously engages in filial sentimentality in another story, "The Golden Cangue," which is fully addressed in chapter 3. Qiqiao 七巧, the heroine, is extremely possessive of her son, Changbai 長白. Qiqiao, married to a disabled husband, craves love and helplessly devotes herself to the son. She spoils him and tortures his wife. When Changbai cooks opium for her, Qiqiao broods about him: all "these years he had been the only man in her life. Only with him there was no danger of his being after her money—it was his anyway. But being her son, he amounted to less than half a man. And even the half she could not keep, now that he was married."[50] Confined within an extremely Confucius domestic setting, Qiqiao has only one outlet to vent her excessive desire, be it sexual or affectionate, and that is the filial connection to her own son. As her son, as well as her only "half a man" in her lonely life, Changbai bizarrely shoulders two roles for Qiqiao. She radically distorts filial love, with which she eventually destroys herself and her own children.

Chang reveals how filial love is potentially led by parents rather than children, and she thereby questions and challenges the misinterpretation embedded in the dominant discourse of filial piety and the global discourse of Freud. In the two stories by Chang, the eccentric passionate love between father and daughter as well as between mother and son is embodied in the distorted filial piety in traditional Chinese culture. In both stories, the filial piety recorded and promoted by the Chinese tradition can serve as a moral disguise for incestuous desire. While it would be unwarranted to argue that filial morality is itself a "displaced incest that celebrates precisely daughters sleeping with fathers,"[51] this filial morality could be exploited to meet selfish, personal desires, thereby serving as an accomplice to incestuous behavior. Chang's story, therefore, becomes a breakthrough for us to see through the glorified tradition of Chinese filial piety, which is a profound cultural problem because of its conflict with the incest prohibition.

Incest Prohibition and Cosmopolitanism

Lawrence's mother-son incestuous desire illustrates an alternative narrative of a deep cultural problem in the West that also drew attention from Freud. As opposed to Freud, Lawrence pins the source of the incestuous desire on the parents rather than the children, thus indicating a deep cultural problem in the modern West. Likewise, Chang's depiction of incestuous desire between a Chinese daughter and her father indicates that the source of the problem is the father who fails to hold onto the incest prohibition. The problem of the family can be extended to the problem of the parental culture that demands a passionate filial piety embedded in traditional Chinese culture. The discourse of filial piety, a lasting morality, contributes to the weakening of the incest prohibition, the first morality of humanity. There seems to be a fundamental contradiction between the morality of incest prohibition and the morality of filial piety. Filial piety can be used as a pretext for the overemphasis on the bond with the parents, leading to the deterioration of the incest prohibition. The relaxing of the incest prohibition creates an obsession with the familiar rather than the foreign. Just as Fengyi and Gertrude are both obsessed with their own desires, their families remain obsessed with themselves and unable to look beyond their own horizons. Such a family dysfunction projects a deep cultural problem: a decline of morality in the parental culture.

The stories demonstrate that the maintenance of the moral order embodied in the incest prohibition is the prerequisite for the ability to create new bonds with the foreign. The ability to engage with the foreign is in turn the basis for cosmopolitanism. We have been told that a globalized society needs to break down cultural boundaries and flatten out local specificities, for instance, through economic globalization and Freud's claim of a universal Oedipus complex. Yet, both Lawrence and Chang argue that the foundation of cosmopolitanism demands a strong local culture that paves the way to form affinities with foreign cultures. When the local culture is as weak and incapable as the parents described by Chang and Lawrence, the only hope for reestablishing the incest prohibition would come from the children.

But if this is the case, then there is a key difference between Chang's and Lawrence's stories because Paul is able to recover the incest prohibition while Xiaohan cannot. This difference stems from the way in which the tradition of filial piety sugarcoats the weakening of the incest prohibition in China. This tradition allows Xiaohan to mistake incestuous desire for paternal love, and she is never able to recognize the incestuous behavior of her father for what it is and is therefore unable to blame him for the incestuous situation. She even attempts to return to her father at the end of the story, trying to displace her friend, Lingqing, as the object of his affections. By contrast, without the deep influence of filial piety, Paul sees the malicious influence that his mother's behavior has on him and makes several attempts to escape her through his relationships with other women. At the end of the story, he must kill her under the pretext of euthanasia in order to escape her. But if Paul is able to carry out this rebellion and Xiaohan cannot, then such a killing of the parent cannot be a universal childhood desire described by the Oedipus complex, which is also inadequate for explaining the son's killing of the mother. Both stories describe the weakening of the incest prohibition as the result of a failure on the part of the parents; but it is only in *Sons and Lovers* that the child is able to recognize the moral weakness in the parent.

Both writers critique the decline of morality in order to liberate people from inward implosion and allow them to seek a potential love with strangers and their cultures. Critiquing the problem of incest in their cultures, Lawrence and Chang see the enforcing of the incest prohibition as the pathway out of the confinements of repressive local cultures and toward a cosmopolitan love. By encouraging love for strangers, the incest prohibition not only regulates family relationships but, in doing so, also establishes the cognitive and cultural basis for a healthy local culture that resists an inward-looking self-obsession and has enough self-confidence to be able to appreciate and engage with another culture in order to eventually link the local with the foreign.

TWO

Sexual Love as Public Defiance

Sexual love, a more developed form of love, characterizes Lawrence's *The Virgin and the Gipsy* and Chang's "Se, jie" 色，戒 ("Lust, Caution"). Although the two works of fiction are written in different styles, in both of them sexual love liberates women, prompting them to defy their local constructions in a context of nationalism and war.

Written in 1926 but published posthumously in 1930, *The Virgin and the Gipsy* was deemed "one of Lawrence's finest things" by the influential Cambridge scholar F. R. Leavis.[1] Chang's "Lust, Caution," written in the 1950s but not published until 1978,[2] also achieved belated fame as an unconventional espionage story set in 1940s Shanghai.[3] It had been excluded for decades from the canon of mainstream modern Chinese literature due to the ironic twist on the nationalist narrative until it was adapted for the screen in 2007 by Ang Lee 李安.[4] Besides achieving a similar level of fame, each work of fiction features a female character who withdraws from her own society to find personal expression elsewhere. In Chang's story, Wang Jiazhi 王佳芝, a Chinese woman nationalist spy during the Sino-Japanese War (1937–45), unexpectedly falls in love with a Chinese traitor, a figure that has been reviled in postwar literature and film. Jiazhi first realizes that she loves the traitor at the very moment when he buys her a rare ring. Similarly, Yvette, the heroine of D. H. Lawrence's *The Virgin and the Gipsy*, falls in love with a gypsy when she first looks closely at his body.[5] She betrays her social class, for the Victorians believed that gypsies were inferior outsiders. Despite their different writing styles, Lawrence's *The Virgin and the Gipsy* and Chang's "Lust, Caution" both embody a powerful defiance that is expressed by sexual love. This chapter investigates the similar sexual defiance communicated by Lawrence and Chang in their narratives and the different moral conventions and nationalist discourses that such defiance attempts to debunk in each society.

53

Lawrence and Chang surprisingly transcend their national limits by elevating private desire to reverse the dominant discourse of nationalism that is defined by norms and conventions. Through a woman's sexual defiance, Lawrence challenges the false morality and social order that define post-Victorian, post–World War I modern England. Chang believes 1940s Chinese society subjugates individuality (gender and sexuality in the case of a woman) in the name of nation building and independence. Refusing to participate in political activities, she nonetheless reshaped modern Chinese culture to make it receptive to individualism. Both authors focus on women's desire in order to challenge public perceptions with private feelings. They depict the way in which sexual love can emancipate women from social conventions that suppress and confine the female body.

Defiant Female Desire

The Virgin and the Gipsy concentrates on a woman's discovery of her sexual desire and primal selfhood. Yvette, a bourgeois young woman, is stifled by her rectory family's false morality and the corrupt social order around them. At the climax of the narrative, she is transfigured by a flood. In his analysis of the novel, Leavis connects the flood with the change in Yvette when he points out "the crucial significance of desire—of vindicating desire in the sense of compelling a clear and clean and reverent recognition."[6] The flood mythically represents Yvette's female desire, a desire for sexual freedom and reverent recognition by the other. Before the climactic flood, the sexual energy of Yvette's primitive desire takes the form of a search for recognition. Yvette is hostile to her family members, who maintain a false morality: the old and blind grandma "with her insatiable greed for life, other people's life"; the pious Aunt Cissie, who is "gnawed by an inward worm"; and her unbelieving father, who recoils when he is faced with the unconventional.[7] Once she is sexually awakened by her encounter with the gypsy, Yvette becomes susceptible to radical change. The flood creates a rare moment when sex and love converge to breed a significant power of sexual love, allowing Lawrence to reward her rebellion against middle-class conventions and argue for the freedom that her encounter with the gypsy represents.

Yvette's personal transformation is depicted in a realistic style that challenges the old moral codes. At first sight, Yvette is obsessed with the gypsy's physicality. She reacts to the feeling of his eyes upon her: "Yvette quivered suddenly, as if she had seen his big, bold eyes upon her, with the naked insinuation of desire in them. The absolutely naked insinuation of desire made her lie prone and powerless in the bed" (30). The thought that the gypsy desires her releases her from the confinement of the rectory, and Yvette is conscious of her own transformation after her encounter with the gypsy. They might have consummated their desire in the caravan had they not been interrupted by the arrival of a car. The failure of their consummation causes sex to step aside and to be erased, but its very absence paradoxically renders sex extraordinarily salient and significant in this love relation. When the gypsy asks Yvette to follow him to the caravan, she "followed simply, followed the silent, secret, overpowering motion of his body in front of her. It cost her nothing. She was gone in his will" (47). Irresistible to her, he utterly captivates her as she falls under his spell. This significant encounter with the gypsy liberates Yvette and transforms her into a new woman.

Lawrence shifts our sights from the male perception of a woman's body to the female's response to a man's body. Nancy Paxton observes, "Yvette offers another example of a modern woman who begins her sexual initiation by watching an attractive man." Rejecting the English conventions that suppressed women's sexuality and individual fulfillment, "Yvette is not punished for her voyeurism or for the relationship she establishes with the gipsy."[8] Through a woman's gaze, Lawrence empowers women to challenge conventional gender roles in order to liberate their sexuality.

Despite the realistic details, a metaphorical attraction, rather than animal instinct, brings about the fulfillment of the interpersonal relation between Yvette and the gypsy. Surprisingly, the gypsy's love for Yvette points to the very existence of mutual love between them. It turns out that when Joe (the gypsy) rescues Yvette from the flood, he actually loves her sincerely and tenderly. Afterward he writes her, in his own broken English, a letter that reveals his true feelings: "I see in the paper you are all right after your ducking. [. . .] I come that day to say Goodbye! and I never said it, well, the water give no time, but I live in hopes" (78).

In Lawrence's novella, sex and love are closely intertwined. However, because Lawrence uses a rather mythical flood to represent whatever consummation takes place between the lovers, critics have naturally wondered whether Yvette loses her virginity. The answer varies among scholars. According to John Turner, for example, it "is not the physical but the spiritual aspect of virginity that counts. The great climax to *The Virgin and the Gipsy* is not the physical but the spiritual embrace of that which had been taboo."[9] It is important that Yvette, saved by the gypsy, achieves her rebirth, freedom, and fulfillment simultaneously in the flood, just as Major Eastwood, sounding like Lawrence, claims that "desire is the most wonderful thing in life" (57). The woman's desire is deeply hidden in this apocalyptic flood. Lawrence's mythical depiction of sexual love leaves space for readers to formulate their own interpretations. The mythical writing would have protected him from censorship if he had chosen to publish the novella. More importantly, his downplaying of the sexuality in sexual love underscores the ambiguity of the relation between sex and love in the story.

Chang adopts another way of subtly indicating sexual love. In "Lust, Caution," she implies that Wang Jiazhi's love for Mr. Yi 易先生, a collaborator with the Japanese puppet government in China, originated with a woman's sexuality, her deepest self. Love in "Lust, Caution" presents itself as abruptly and mysteriously at the very end as does the flood at the end of *The Virgin and the Gipsy*. At the very moment when he is to be assassinated, Mr. Yi buys Jiazhi a pink diamond ring, a symbolic promise of happiness. In the otherworldly jewelry shop, Jiazhi sinks into contemplation and slips into a dreamlike state. This implicitly reveals the sexuality that generates love. Jiazhi in the jewelry shop exemplifies other people's definition of love: love is connected to power, and "the way to a women's heart is through her vagina."[10] Even though rejecting this saying as something vulgar, Jiazhi finds herself "unable to refute that notion [that she is in love with Mr. Yi] entirely."[11] While she is entirely alone in the store with Mr. Yi and can see his sad but tenderly affectionate contemplation,[12] Jiazhi suddenly realizes that her love for Mr. Yi is true. The ring here symbolizes a desirable, genuine, indestructible, and permanent love for which Jiazhi's private self has been pining during the cruel war, in which all the nationalists were indifferent to private feelings. "He really loves me, she thought. Inside, she felt a raw tremor of shock—then a vague sense of loss. It was too late. [. . .] 'Run,' she said softly."[13] She saves her lover at this instant when the feeling of true love shocks and awakens her deepest self. Nicole Huang comments, "At this critical moment [. . .] it is her innermost feelings that become clearer. Her longing for connectedness and intimacy is brought to the foreground, under the dreamy orange light of the jewelry store, while her moral and national obligations recede into the dark background."[14] Jiazhi discovers love, recognizes her innermost self, and liberates her female desire from the confinement of Confucian morality and national commitment in this perilous liaison.

Jiazhi's transformation is deeply rooted in her sexual love. Her individual search for mutual recognition is through sexual love regardless of political agenda. Like Yvette, she becomes aware of her body, heart, and self. However, this awareness is delayed. During the period of her sexual experiences with Mr. Yi, she develops feelings for him that build up even though she remains unaware of them. She only recognizes the love when she is given a rare diamond that represents his commitment to her. Eventually, sexuality converges with love to breed a sexual love that dramatically changes the meaning of the whole story.

The traitor, saved and alerted, quickly ends the assassination plot by killing everyone involved, including his lover. Yet, Mr. Yi also confesses his real feeling for Jiazhi after making the decision to execute her. Jiazhi's psychology in the jewelry store and Mr. Yi's reflection on his possessive and passionate love at the end of the story both demonstrate the rare value of a sexual love between the two lovers. After executing Jiazhi, Mr. Yi ponders, "He had enjoyed the love of a beautiful woman, he could die happy—without regret. He could feel her shadow forever near him, comforting him. [. . .] And now he possessed her utterly, primitively—as a hunter does his quarry, a tiger his kill. Alive, her body belonged to him; dead, she was his ghost."[15] His extremely primitive desire for Jiazhi echoes her previous thought about the connection between love and the vagina. The sexual desire evolves into a passionate love to which Jiazhi could sacrifice her life and within which Mr. Yi would crave the eternal possession of his lover. Although he must end Jiazhi's life under complicated circumstances, Mr. Yi also confesses that the idea of executing her (the death, the ultimate violence) is interconnected with the urge to possess her eternally, which echoes Jiazhi's attraction to render their relationship mutual and serious.

Ang Lee dramatically depicts the underlying erotic desire in his NC-17-rated film.[16] Lee boldly and explicitly visualizes the sensual desire that Chang carefully and covertly portrayed. He perceives the sexual relation between the heroine and her lover as sadomasochistic. "[Chang] revised the story for years and years—for decades—returning to it as a criminal might return to the scene of a crime, or as a victim might reenact a trauma, reaching for pleasure only by varying and reimagining the pain."[17] Lee's unique understanding is evidence for my contention that the story emphasizes sexual desire. As Hsiu-Chuang Deppman observes in her comparative studies of Ang Lee and Eileen Chang, Lee "deepens our understanding of Chang's philosophy, style, and aesthetic."[18] Lee presents his intensely erotic cinematic vision in a way that resonates with the sexual tension in Chang's literary imagination.

Jiazhi's love seems mystical since Chang does not explicitly elaborate on the question of the source of the love. This mysticism may arise in part from censorship, which was a similar factor in Lawrence's mythic writing. Chang only hints at sex because she acknowledges the taboos in publishing. Publishers in the 1950s always avoided openly mentioning sex. Later, she offered a shockingly explicit depiction of sexual desire in *The Little Reunion* (*Xiao tuanyuan* 小團圓, 2009), written in the United States between 1975 and 1976. Censorship in the 1970s was not as restrictive as in the 1950s, partially due to the triumphant reception of Lawrence's *Lady Chatterley's Lover* in 1960. Indeed, censorship is an easy and convenient way to explain both the obliqueness of Chang's depiction of sex and Lawrence's mythological treatment of it.

However, beneath the symbolic mode of writing in both Chang and Lawrence lies the ambiguity of the relation between love and sex in the stories. For Lawrence, it is certain that Yvette and the gypsy love each other, but sex is highly ambiguous, even in the final scene of the flood. Their sexual consummation has been held in suspense over the course of the narrative. The absence of sex, however, enlarges and strengthens its significance in the final scene in which love can utterly replace sex. It does not matter whether or not the virgin and the gypsy eventually have sex because love equates to sex at the slipping and precious moment of encounter.

In contrast, Chang explicitly reveals the existence of sex between Jiazhi and Mr. Yi regardless of the omission of sex scenes. Love is quite evasive and uncertain compared to the open existence of sex in the story. The only moment in which sex equates to love is when Jiazhi looks at the pink ring that Mr. Yi is buying for her. Observing the gift of love, Jiazhi links love to sex in her stream of consciousness in the jewelry store. She sacrifices herself to save her lover before the imminent assassination. This moment of enlightenment is crucial because the disclosure of sexual love is held in suspension over a long period of time in which Jiazhi was weaponizing sex in order to manipulate Mr. Yi. Such a temporal displacement of sexual love demonstrates the difficulty in reinterpreting the meaning of sex to arrive at love.

When Jiazhi is imagining and envisioning true love, sex and love encounter each other and create a fleeting moment of rare utopian love, which is deeply meaningful. Because this utopian vision results in a change in Jiazhi's understanding of herself and by extension her political identity, the fulfilling moment of sexual love marks her dramatic participation in politics. With an expectation of utopian love ahead, Jiazhi transforms her understanding of sex in a way that brings sex out of the realm of private experience and transports it into a discursive realm, which is immediately public. In that moment she realizes that sexual love is defining for the self, which gains autonomy and freedom. The private only becomes public through an act of reinterpretation that is driven by the longing for love and culminates in the establishment of sexual love.

Likewise, at the end of Lawrence's novella, love presents itself in a utopian moment. If the flood represents mythical sex, then the letter the gypsy writes to Yvette fulfills a sexual love. The letter establishes mutual recognition and affection by discursively recasting sexual desire as a human bond. At the very last moment, the sexual love reveals itself as something that transcends class and ethnic boundaries, thereby entering into public discourse.

The imbalanced ratio of sex and love in the structure of these narratives reveals an alternative understanding of sexual love that is dramatically opposed to a definition of sexual love in which sex and love are naturally integrated and intertwined. Both Lawrence and Chang propose a sexual love in which the linkage between sex and love is extremely delicate and unstable. Therefore, they emphasize the ultimate value of sexual love because it is very rare and ephemeral for sex and love to converge and equate with each other. The precious coincidence of sex and love creates a utopian moment that transforms sex into the sexual love that releases the power of a private feeling so that it engages with public discourse.

Subversive Cultural Expressions from the Private to the Public

Irving Singer comments on Lawrence's depiction of desire, stating that "Lawrence means more than merely sexual impulse. He also means the desire to exist, to assert one's self, to live in accordance with one's nature, to sense one's instinctual being and to gratify it."[19] By depicting a genuine desire that is inherently sexual and primordial, Lawrence denies the rigid Victorian conventions and the devastating postwar, money-driven industrialism of his time. He renounces modern civilization because he believes civilization is antilife. His desire to negate the cerebral is mythically embodied in the flood at the end of *The Virgin and the Gipsy*. As Kingsley Widmer observes, "Lawrence desperately wants us, and himself, to *feel* differently, and clearly emphasizes that a change in feelings can change the world."[20]

Lawrence and Chang strip their heroines of any social commitments to prevent them from having a fully social existence. Lawrence's Yvette refuses her social role as an obedient daughter and an angelic wife in her bourgeois society. Chang's Jiazhi betrays her patriotic cause and surrenders to her authentic feeling. The two authors affirm personal desire and sincere emotion in the private sphere. Their indulgence in the intimate self and their reluctance to reconcile the intimate and the public demonstrate their distrust of society and authority. The significance and primacy of their sexual defiance can be extended beyond the personal realm to social life as a whole when sex converges with love to transform existing relationships. Their apolitical stance became problematic once they declared their lack of interest in politics. Yet, the moment they affirmed their apathy toward politics they were already participating in the discourse of politics.

Lawrence and Chang both developed defiant forms of desire to target conventions. However, differences in their local realities made it necessary to point to details of the two cultures as crystallized in the stories. The distinctiveness of the moral conventions in each culture led to different structures of subjective desire and corresponding differences in collective national identity. Lawrence and Chang reacted to the modern definition of national identity by liberating women's desire from any conventional confinement, thereby dissolving the hegemonic conventions in their local cultures upon which nationalism was based in the first half of the twentieth century.

Behind Yvette's sexual desire is Lawrence's attempt to subvert the false morality of the rectory that Yvette's family represents. The false morality leads to Victorian pride, nationalism, and British colonialism. In the narrative of a typical English young woman rebelling against familial convention and morality, Lawrence critiques Englishness and the nationalism behind it. Likewise, Chang's immersion within private experience and her seemingly apolitical stance demonstrate her insistence on individualism. Her devotion to the theme of sexual love as the most heightened state of existence in "Lust, Caution" subtly but persistently unsettles the enduring Confucian ideology and the dominant nationalist discourse.[21] Lawrence and Chang both broke the tight connection between love and politics, or, more specifically, desire and nationalism, to channel love back to its hyper-individual domain. Woman's desire, therefore, undermines nationalism because Lawrence and Chang reduce and emancipate passionate love from the regular formula of nationalism: nation plus love.

As significant cultural critics in their respective historical times, they voiced similar responses to different local realities of nation building. In the 1920s, the old Englishness bolstered by preexisting Victorian values, national pride, and rigid class hierarchy was challenged by the frenzied postwar psyche and the fierce class struggles of labor strikes following the 1917 Bolshevik Revolution. Lawrence experienced a changing, wavering, and contradictory worldview during this time. His works also carry a conflicting impulse that may help explain the extremely divided criticism of Lawrence. Gerald's suicide in *Women in Love*, published in 1920, expresses Lawrence's disapproval of a conventional society. In contrast, his last long novel, *Lady Chatterley's Lover*, published in 1928, delivers a strong utopian sense of voluptuous vitality. Similarly, *The Virgin and the Gipsy* expresses the same positive flow of energy and life, which, as Lawrence believes, can be acquired through radical individualism.

This individualism in *The Virgin and the Gipsy* becomes apparent in the way that a woman's sexual love defies Victorian asceticism and Christian morality. As morality was set "in collision with sexuality, the idealizing impulses of Victorian domesticity point to the culmination of Victorian asceticism," as James Adams observes.[22] From the time of the religious revival of the late eighteenth-century Evangelical movement, sexuality was a constant target of attack in Christian morality. Christianity had been the "dominant sexual authority" before the Victorian era.[23]

Through the critique of the rectory's bourgeois class values in *The Virgin and the Gipsy*, Lawrence challenges the rigid Christian morality that was interwoven with oppressive Victorian conventions. Yvette finds her home, supposedly pure and civil, nonetheless filthy, sordid, and repulsive. She thinks her suitor is boring and "beastly" (10). She is horrified by the "parasitic agedness" of her grandmother, or Mater, who represents the ossified social order (31). The rectory, which "smelt of Granny," has the same agedness, uncleanness, and sordidness. Like the old woman, it "seemed ugly, and almost sordid, with the dank air of that middle-class, degenerated comfort which has ceased to be comfortable and has turned stuffy, unclean [. . .] nothing was fresh" (10).

Yvette's profound disgust at the sordid and aged rectory represents Lawrence's hostility toward false morality and puritanical convention. As an acknowledged emblem of Christianity, the rectory represents "the morality of the slaves."[24] Lawrence's modified repetitiveness describes the repulsiveness of the rectory compared to the gypsy's clean quarry. "She hated the rectory, and everything it implied. The whole stagnant, sewerage sort of life, where sewerage is never mentioned, but where it seems to smell from the centre of every two-legged inmate, from Granny to the servants, was foul. If gipsies had no bathrooms, at least they had no sewerage. There was fresh air" (29–30). Repulsed by the stifling social order represented by the Mater and the rectory, Lawrence symbolically washes away Granny and the rectory in the mythical flood.

In contrast to the repulsiveness of the world Yvette belongs to, the gypsy is pure, clean, and potent. When Yvette meets the gypsy's eyes, "something hard in her registered the peculiar pure lines of his face, of his straight, pure nose, of his cheeks and temples. The curious dark, suave purity of all his body, outlined in the green jersey: a purity like a living sneer" (24). This passage about the purity of the gypsy's body reflects Lawrence's rebellion against the false purity of English society at the time. David Craig observes that "as one who led the revolt against the long Victorian regime of strict taboo on the discussion of intimate experience, Lawrence was bitterly against the cults of innocence, 'purity', and self-sacrifice at the expense of passional fulfilment."[25] True morality, for Lawrence, is based on life. After Yvette visits the gypsy's camp, she feels as if "the thought of the gipsy had released the life of her limbs, and crystalized in her heart the hate of the rectory: so that now she felt potent, instead of impotent" (30). Yvette's attraction to the gypsy's body illustrates Lawrence's worship of life. The word "potent" strongly indicates sex and life, which are the vitalizing force of reproduction. Moreover, according to John Reed, the character of the gypsy symbolizes freedom and "a reawakened life" in Victorian literary conventions.[26] Lawrence adopts this image of the gypsy, who is full of life and emancipates Yvette from the stifling old world of the dying.

Yvette desires and loves Joe, the gypsy, just as Constance (Connie) Chatterley in *Lady Chatterley's Lover* loves Mellors, the gamekeeper. Both Connie and Yvette rebel against social convention and transgress class boundaries in order to consummate their primitive forms of love. As Drew Milne observes, "The search for recognition through love and sex becomes a key form of the difficulty of class consciousness, combining both a sense of the physical needs understood as sexuality and the more mental forms of mutual recognition associated with love."[27] By glorifying a radical sexual communion between a lower-class man and a privileged lady in the private domain, Lawrence dissolves the lasting structure of class upon which British nationalism was founded.

Compared to Lawrence's radical individualism at odds with his society, Chang's individualism, as expressed in the heroine's sexual self, is conveyed with less confidence and aggression in a situation where Confucianism and nationalism had absolute power over individuals. The difference derives from the diverging attitudes toward individualism in Western and Chinese cultures. It is commonly acknowledged that Western societies have greatly valued individuality since the Renaissance. Countless thinkers, including Michel de Montaigne, John Locke, Thomas Jefferson, and Friedrich Nietzsche, have conceptualized individualism in Western history through their emphasis on individual rights, free thought, self-interest, and subjectivity. The radical individualists, like Lawrence, even believe that individualism precedes the community and the nation. Lawrence illustrates this individualism in *The Virgin and the Gipsy* by depicting Yvette as a woman with independent thoughts and feelings, pursuing her own desire and privileging sexual love over her class. By contrast, in the 1940s the idea of individualism was still alien to the conventional Chinese mind, which invoked Confucianism and modern nationalism in order to insist that everything must be subjugated to the nation.

To find a way past conventional thinking, Chang develops the trope of female espionage, which complies with but in the end abruptly subverts the traditional mode of thinking about women and the state. Jiazhi becomes a spy to undermine the political enemy, though she is not the first female spy in Chinese culture. Politicians used women as "honey traps" throughout Chinese history. Two famous beauties in ancient China, Xi Shi 西施 and Diao Chan 貂蟬, used their beauty and stratagems to assist in the defeat of political enemies. Xi Shi was a gift from King Goujian of Yue in 490 BC to King Fuchai of Wu so that King Fuchai would indulge himself in her beauty, which would leave himself vulnerable to Yue's attack. Diao Chan in the end of the Eastern Han dynasty (25–220 AD) was assigned to sow discord between the tyrant Dong Zhuo 董卓 and his foster son Lü Bu 呂布. Nevertheless, Chang's heroine does not act as a pawn between men in highly masculine political conspiracies. In the traditional Confucian mode of thinking, women were supposed to submit strictly to a set of moral principles, three obediences and four virtues, which require a woman to obey her father before marriage, her husband when married, and her son in widowhood, as well as to stay virtuous in morality, speech, manner, and wifely work. Jiazhi was unconsciously trying to think and behave as a firm believer in the traditional Chinese ideologies. However, her primordial self constantly bubbles up and disturbs the Confucian discourse of women's subjugation and suppression.

Besides opposing the preexisting Confucian morality that defined China as a state, Chang also distanced herself from the overarching sociopolitical ethos shared by mainstream May Fourth intellectuals, such as Lu Xun 魯迅 and Mao Dun 茅盾. China had endured invasions and exploitation from Western countries since the 1840s. In the 1940s, when Chang wrote most of her successful love stories in Shanghai, China was enduring the second Sino-Japanese War (1937–45). Many Chinese writers in twentieth-century China, starting with Liang Qichao 梁啟超 and Kang Youwei 康有為, intermixed politics with art and even subjected art to the cause of political revolution. The May Fourth intellectuals, the leftists, and the communists all attempted to use literature as an effective, manipulative means to evoke patriotic impulses, to mobilize people to overthrow the imperial domination of Confucian authority, and to radically transform China into a progressive, modern nation. China, motivated by a sweeping revolutionary drive, resolutely subordinated anything individual, including gender, sexuality, ethnicity, and feelings, to the absolute political cause. Nationalism was privileged over individualism and gender in all facets of society and literary life. Women writers risked being discounted by leftist intellectuals for persistently centering on domestic matters; thus they also devoted themselves to the revolutionary cause as their male counterparts did.[28] Ding Ling 丁玲 (1904–86), one such outstanding woman writer, is an excellent example. She boldly explored women's subjectivity and sexuality in her early career but drastically converted to the nationalist cause, afterward focusing on depictions of national turmoil and social engagement.[29]

Contrary to this highly politicized, utilitarian modern Chinese literature, Chang's discordant voice antagonizes as a counter-discourse to modern nationalism. Chang never engaged with the big historical picture in the 1940s or bought into the patriotic aura as other Chinese writers did in such a time of social upheaval. Leo Ou-fan Lee, in his innovative effort to study Shanghai urban culture, addresses Chang's "Cassandra-like stance" in her stories, "as it runs counter to the prevailing ethos of nationalism and revolutionary progress at the time."[30] Similarly, Julia Lovell writes: "In 'Lust, Caution', the loud, public questions—war, revolution, national survival—that Chang had for decades been accused of sidelining are freely given centre stage, then exposed as transient, alienating, and finally subordinate to the quiet, private themes of emotional loyalty, vanity and betrayal."[31] Chang dramatized political upheaval as a means to interpret the theme of love and personal salvation rather than to promote national salvation. In this sense, Chang shares Lawrence's skepticism toward war and collective nationalism.

Just as Yvette hates the rectory, in "Lust, Caution" Jiazhi disdains politics, and her preference for love over politics serves as a dissenting note in the prevailing leitmotif of nationalism in early twentieth-century China. As Julia Lovell puts it, "Chang created for the first time a heroine directly swept up in the radical, patriotic politics of the 1940s, charting her exploitation in the name of nationalism and her impulsive abandonment of the cause for an illusory love."[32] Though Lovell calls the love "illusory," Chang subtly and dryly asserts that anything individual is more meaningful and important than patriotism and nationalism. Jiazhi liberates herself from political enslavement and achieves "the freedom of her real self," as Whitney Crothers Dilley asserts in her study of the "real" Wang Jiazhi.[33] Like the heroine in the story, Chang views sexual love (women's subjectivity and sexuality in this story) as the most genuine and ultimate form of self-expression and individualism. The discourse of love and sexuality, therefore, is released from politics and nationalism to exist as a legitimate subject on its own.

Some critics believe that Chang's influence was constrained to merely private, domestic spheres because of her self-proclaimed apolitical stance. However, this apolitical stance surprisingly functions as an effective means to reverse the cultural hierarchy and can consequently be understood as an effort to engage in "lowercase-p" politics.[34] Her works contributed to the Chinese revolution of sexuality and heart and added a strikingly different dimension to modern Chinese history. Nicole Huang believes that Chang was seeking "channels of self-expression at an adverse time, to tell a different sort of wartime story, and, most importantly, to challenge the existing literary hierarchy and establish a new literary order."[35] Because of a small number of modern writers such as Eileen Chang, individualism in the form of women's subjectivity, sexuality, and love has been gradually elevated to a higher level in the cultural hierarchy in contemporary China. More importantly, individualism in the form of woman's desire establishes a primacy of love over politics in China's local culture to create a realm of freedom.

Unique Authorial Intentions behind the Female Gaze

Besides the dissimilar conventions that shaped each author, different worldviews inform their distinctive literary narratives about women and individualism. Amplifying the woman's gaze, Lawrence and Chang both focus on female desire. Each story represents a female viewpoint that disturbs and disrupts the masculine discourse about women's bodies and sexuality. Both authors looked for ways to articulate what we see today as a feminist point of view. However, different authorial intentions are found behind the seemingly similar feminist awareness. This disparity comes to light in the images of women in their narratives. Jiazhi and Yvette differ a great deal if one delves into the details. Jiazhi has conformed to her social role until her last-minute awakening, while Yvette discovers her sexual self in the beginning and consistently works toward her self-emancipation. Jiazhi's preference for her bodily and emotional self comes at the cost of her life, while Yvette's rebellion is rewarded with the gypsy's act of lifesaving. Whether Jiazhi's desire was attained or denied remains perplexingly ambivalent, but it is clear that Yvette is empowered by her newly discovered sexuality and worldliness. In contrast to Yvette's gypsy, Jiazhi's lover terminates her awakened self-knowledge, her promised love, and her life. Her death ironically perpetuates women's marginalization, bodily effacement, and endless struggle for their own power in a male-dominated society. Chang's "Lust, Caution" is as much a discourse about powerlessness as it is about power. As Haiyan Lee observes, "It is notoriously difficult to discern lines of oppression and victimization in Chang's fictional world. Invidious hierarchies of class, gender, and race are omnipresent, and yet they intersect in such a way as to diffuse any possibility of righteous indignation, unalloyed compassion, or solidarity-making."[36] The story is as much about submission as it is about sexual and emotional fulfillment.

Chang complicates and problematizes Jiazhi's self-sacrificial love, unveiling the tension between individual desire and state politics. An awakened woman ready to pursue her individual fulfillment is constantly threatened by unreconciled social expectations about women's sex and gender. The ambiguity concerning female desire, achieved or frustrated, problematizes the dichotomy between the private and the public in a revolutionary culture. On the one hand, as a woman, Chang was aware of the powerful suppressions that women encountered and experienced in early twentieth-century China as a result of Confucianism and patriotism. On the other hand, it was more difficult for Chang to revolt than for Lawrence, who was born into a working class family. As one of the last aristocrats from the Qing dynasty brought up in a traditional family but exposed to Western education, Chang could not completely betray traditional moral principles, nor could she embrace the radical patriotic dogma that ended the final empire. This ambivalence explains the irresolution and vacillation presented by Chang's heroines, including Jiazhi. Chang's story ends with the failure of a woman's pursuit of emotional fulfillment.

Compared to Chang's frustrated attempt to liberate women from the demands of nationalism, Lawrence extends his critique directly toward social order rather than merely cultural politics by injecting his heroic, vigorous, and triumphant spirit into his representation of women and sexuality. Despite the harsh attacks from Simone de Beauvoir and Kate Millet cited in the introduction, Lawrence's discourse about women is more complex and positive than it sometimes seems. As Carol Siegel observes, Lawrence's work seems "too fluid, changeable, and even self-contradictory to fit this developmental pattern, especially when one considers that *The Virgin and the Gipsy*, written in 1926, has in common with intentionally feminist texts like *Jane Eyre* a concern with combating the negative connotation traditionally given to female flow."[37] Lawrence's female characters and their primitive desires deserve a more sensitive appreciation. With a different perspective from Chang's gynocentricism, Lawrence intensely engaged with sociopolitical problems. However, the hopelessly fallen world troubled by war, money-driven industrialism, labor strikes, and obsolete moral conventions disheartened and frustrated Lawrence. He took a radically utopian leap by retreating into the private sphere, where he believed life and regeneration were possible and radical individualism could offer an alternative solution to the problems of the outside world.

The seemingly domestic topic of women and sexuality actually embodies Lawrence's ambition to address sociopolitical issues. Lawrence believed women, sexuality, and the communion between man and woman could offer a utopian transcendence of the bleak situation. "For Lawrence, the female, although it is said to be coeval with the male, would seem to be the more primitive. It is, radically, the maternal element of origins which are of the flesh and of the blood. As such, it is further associated with darkness—the darkness of the womb and of birth," as Baruch Hochman observes.[38] Indeed, to Lawrence, women and womb serve as the path to the regeneration of the world. His depiction of rebellious women and liberating sexual relations is a response to the sociopolitical tensions and problems in his time. In this sense, his literary attention was primarily drawn to larger social and even cosmic questions rather than to the gender struggle that concerned Chang. It devalues Lawrence if we merely evaluate him in terms of a feminist cultural agenda.

Shutting out the overwhelming noise of politics, Chang was concerned with women's subjectivity and gender relations in the private sphere.

Depicting the conflict within family and love, Lawrence sought to question the social order. Set against Chang, Lawrence seems more determined and aggressive in his cultural critique. His heroines are therefore rendered as strong and invincible. Yvette never submits. The mythical flood charged with an irresistible sexual power destroys the old world and creates a new possibility. Yet, his great leap of literary imagination from a dystopian England to an enlightening man-woman sexual love can be a utopian vision for the West, compared to Chang's cold, pessimistic but realistic depiction of a depressing Chinese society. Chang experimented in different ways from Lawrence and moved away from sociopolitical expectations, thereby indicating her latent resistance to social conventions in both Confucianism and nationalism.

Lawrence endeavored to release English literature from sexual suppression by depicting intense relationships driven by sexual desire stemming from the deepest self. Depicting women as real people with sexuality and love, Lawrence had a great impact on sexual freedom, freedom of the press, and the beginning of the second wave of feminism in the latter part of the twentieth century. As a male writer who was concerned about social conventions and politics, Lawrence adopted the subversive power of sexual love to rebel against the prevailing false morality and class hierarchy that defined British nationalism in the early twentieth century. As for Chang, individualism, embodied in women's subjectivity, feelings, and sexual love, elegantly and covertly eroded the Chinese discourse of nationalism in the first half of the twentieth century. This mode of individualism was passed on to numerous modern and contemporary Chinese writers, such as Li Ang, Shi Shuqing, Zhong Xiaoyang, and Wang Anyi. All these Chang-school writers develop the themes of women and love in conjunction with individualism.

The Virgin and the Gipsy and "Lust, Caution" highlight sexual love as a road to freedom, even if the freedom never arrives with certainty. Both works assert woman's desire and regenerated selfhood in rebellion against the dehumanizing social orders in their nationalistic cultures. This power of defiance deconstructs local authority and moral rigidity and further carves out more space for genuine feeling and active political engagement. If the critique of incestuous love described in chapter 1 represents the struggle to break the shackles of an oppressive and immoral family culture, the affirmation of sexual love finds a way to reach a realm of freedom that is briefly achieved through a utopian moment that coincides with the cosmopolitan transcendence of national boundaries.

THREE

Adulterous Love as Modern Creation

When sexual passion finds itself outside of the marriage, it transforms into a transgressive love that institutionally challenges the local and global norms of modernization. In *Lady Chatterley's Lover* (1928) Lawrence tells a story of modern adultery that crosses boundaries of class, convention, and ideology in industrial England. Chang's comparable story of transgression, "Jinsuo ji" 金鎖記 ("The Golden Cangue") (1943), unveils a tragedy of a low-class woman married to, but also imprisoned in, the "golden cangue," a disabled husband in a wealthy family. (In old China, a cangue was a giant block of wood locked around the neck of a criminal.) Lawrence celebrates the consummation of the adulterous love, while Chang pessimistically denies the fulfillment of the woman's love. For Chang, an unhappy marriage, failed adultery, and extreme loneliness lead to the heroine's evilness, madness, and eventual violence against others.

One can easily argue that adultery can be understood as a modern relationship because it dissolves traditional bonds. Flaubert's *Madame Bovary* shows that a traditional middle-class marriage cannot sustain an emotional pursuit of extraordinariness in the form of an irrational craving for material abundance. However, adultery in Lawrence and Chang is an antimodern relationship because the traditional bonds are themselves now modern forms of relationship that exclude love. The structure of modernity is still built upon the preexisting traditional norms in England and China, thereby breeding alienation and disconnection. Hence, the prevailing forms of relationship are so suffused with modern alienation that only adultery can be a pure form of love that opposes this alienation. Adulterous love surpasses, undermines, and destroys the existing order to set up an alternative basis for modern society.

Both Lawrence and Chang react against the globalized discourse of modernity in their distinctive ways.[1] Lawrence uses mythical scenes and symbolic characters to oppose the cold intellectualism and mechanical industrialism of modern civilization. His discourse, thus, is dialectic. Love, warm and organic, serves as the antidote to the West's modern insanity. Chang, by contrast, reveals the desolation of modernity through what she calls "de-cadenced contrast (*cenci de duizhao* 參差的對照)."[2] This is her term for the contrast between an envisioned true love and the internal destructiveness of utilitarian Chinese pragmatism. The result is the aesthetics of desolation, which reacts against the dominant discourse of modernization in China.

Lady Chatterley's Lover begins with Connie's feeling of emptiness after her husband, Sir Clifford, becomes impotent during World War I. She struggles in Wragby, her husband's home and also an industrial colliery. In an isolated hut in the woods, Connie is awakened by sexual fulfillment with Mellors, the gamekeeper. Their love begins with a compassionate tenderness that later develops into a deep sexual communication. Pregnant with Mellors's child, Connie leaves Clifford and embarks on a new journey. The ending indicates the very possible marriage of Connie and Mellors. The antagonism between Clifford and Connie/Mellors embodies the conflict between two different ideologies: mind, intellectualism, mechanism, and money-driven industrial insanity versus body, warm sensuality, organic interpersonal relation, and anti-civilizational anarchy. This conflict is a symbolic one that structures the entire novel. Isolated adulterous love that is filled with bodily warmth, tenderness, and life is the solution prescribed by Lawrence to the postwar modern insanity in the West.

Different from Lawrence's Connie, Chang's lonely wife always waits and is both victim and persecutor, trapped in a time capsule in which the hope for love slowly withers. In "The Golden Cangue," Qiqiao 七巧, from a low-class sesame oil–making family, is married to the second son in the wealthy, high-ranking Jiang (Chiang) family—because this son is an invalid. Nursing her deformed husband and giving birth to two children, Qiqiao is frustrated and gradually exhibits the dark side of her nature, yet she is still genuine and innocent while in love. She is attracted to the third son of the Jiang family, Jize 季澤, who is an unworthy womanizer. Even as he flirts with Qiqiao, Jize refuses to develop a liaison with her because her bad temper and their semi-incestuous family relation will expose him disgracefully. Therefore, Qiqiao's only hope resides in her portion of the legacy, which will secure her financial independence someday in the future. One day, this dream comes true after her husband and her mother-in-law pass away. Jize "confesses" his love after Qiqiao is financially independent. In the name of love, Jize attempts to win Qiqiao's trust in order to gain money from her. Discovering that the real intention behind Jize's love confession is to swindle her, Qiqiao hysterically condemns him and drives him out of her house. Her madness and evilness reveal themselves throughout the rest of her loveless life. She maliciously and insanely manipulates her son and daughter and ruins their lives.

Depicting adulterous love between man and woman, Lawrence and Chang examine public psychology in each of their modern societies through individual psychology. In both Lawrence and Chang, the wife, unsatisfied with her disabled husband, seeks love outside a suffocating marital life to breathe the air of freedom. The woman's impulse for love and the subsequent act of adultery represent the writer's defiance against the institutionalized logic of modern rationality in each of their local cultures as well as the global momentum of modernization. For Lawrence, adulterous love becomes sacred and truthful when it breaks the structure of a money-driven, deathly modernity in the West. For Chang, the link between adulterous love and modernity is not as direct. Chang is skeptical toward both traditional arranged marriage and individual choice of marriage partners. Consequently, her text depicts a desolation that reflects her anxiety about radical cultural changes during the transition period from Confucian to modern China. The frustrated adulterous love and the ensuing violence indirectly express her anxiety toward a bleak modernity in China.

The Aristocratic Wife's Victorious Betrayal

The love triangle in Lawrence's story directly symbolizes the conflict between an organic emotional connectedness and a modernity whose logic is hyperrationality and money-driven industrialization. For Lawrence, a deathly modernity, inheriting cold intellectualism and rigid order from traditional Englishness, results in the disconnection between man and woman in Western society; by contrast, it is the primeval sexual union that can reestablish an organic bond that can counter the rigid structure of Western modernity. Consciously extending the private sphere to the public, Lawrence instills his major arguments into Connie's and Mellors's speeches and psychologies. The final victory achieved by Connie and Mellors is Lawrence's triumphant announcement of his own philosophy and also his argument against the modern social diseases incarnated primarily by Clifford. Lawrence portrays his characters not by concrete attributes, such as clothes, facial expressions, and social events, but by their lengthy speeches and psychology. Clifford and his beliefs represent the prevalent ideologies advocated by modern society: reason, mind, industry, and capitalism. For Lawrence, this modernity is genealogically rooted in the traditional norms of England. Clifford, born into an aristocratic class, evolves into an industrial tycoon and represents a modernity that inherits the traditional structure of economy, class, convention, and alienated interrelationship. In the beginning of the novel, Clifford and Connie are occupied by Clifford's work, living a life that is highly intellectual but empty. "Connie had been now nearly two years at Wragby, living this vague life of absorption in Clifford and his needing her, and his work, especially his work. Their interests had never ceased to flow together, over his work. They talked and wrestled in the throes of composition, and felt as if something were happening, really, in the void."[3] He and Connie "lived in their ideas and his books" (19). This absolute rationality is stiff and cold. As Connie reflects upon Clifford and his generation, "They were all inwardly hard and separate, and warmth to them was just bad taste" (72).

Lawrence uses Connie's voice to argue and express his own opinion about empty intellectualism. Connie ponders when she and Clifford take a walk in the woods: "As the years drew on, it was the fear of nothingness in her life that affected her. Clifford's mental life, and hers—gradually it began to feel like nothingness. [. . .] It was words, just so many words" (50). After observing her body in the mirror one night, she realizes the meaninglessness of the body in such a spiritual non-existence and turns her helplessness to fierce hatred. "The mental life! Suddenly she hated it with a rushing fury, the swindle!" (71).

Clifford's rigid rationality and intellectualism are fiercely challenged by Connie's and Mellors's warm bodies and lovemaking. The body functions as the exterior form of blood-consciousness. When Connie glances at Mellors's body as he showers, she appraises the body as warmth and life: "a certain lambency, the warm white flame of a single life revealing itself in contours that one might touch: a body!" (66). Later on, sexually awakened, Connie asks Mellors to give her the "democracy of touch" (73), "the resurrection of the body" (75–76). Not only the whole body but the parts of the body are repeatedly highlighted by Lawrence, who uses words such as "womb" (66), "female blood" (113), "cunt" (177), "woman's arse" (265), "balls" (196), and "penis" (211).

For Lawrence, body is life, opposed to the prosaic, suppressing, and deathly aspects of civilization. In response to Clifford's praise of the "life of the mind" and his disparaging statement that "the life of the body is just the life of the animals," Connie tells him how the body and blood-consciousness have been suppressed in the West: "With the Greeks it gave a lovely flicker, then Plato and Aristotle killed it, and Jesus finished it off" (234–35). She then declares that "now the body is coming really to life, it is really rising from the tomb. And it will be a lovely, lovely life in the lovely universe, the life of the human body" (235). The antithesis between the mind and the body pervades Lawrence's arguments in his other works. In "Democracy," he claims that "you can have life two ways. Either everything is created from the mind, downwards: or else everything proceeds from the creative quick, outwards into foliage and blossom." "The only thing man has to trust to in coming to himself is his desire and his impulse."[4] Lawrence battles against the coldness of the mind, the "upper centre," and attempts to revive and resurrect the warmth of the body. Sex, the culmination of the sensuality and feeling carried by the body, is the antidote to cold intellectualism.

By contrast, Clifford and his property, Wragby colliery, both represent modern industry, which is mechanical, money driven, and deadly. When Clifford finds that intellectualism cannot fulfill him, he regains his power as a man in his industrial cause, the Wragby colliery. Industrialization is actually founded upon the social relations stemming from a pre-existing order, as Clifford evolves from an aristocrat into a coal industry owner. Connie's adultery therefore challenges both tradition and modernization. Lawrence writes of Clifford, "*Now* life came into him! He had been gradually dying, with Connie, in the isolated private life of the artist and the conscious being. [. . .] The very stale air of the colliery was better than oxygen to him. It gave him a sense of power, power [. . .] a man's victory" (108). In industrial society, people blindly pursue money and success by abandoning nature and love. In fact, Clifford's dependence upon the potent industrial machine indicates the connection between cold intellectualism and modern industrialism. Ian Gregor points out, "It is the machine which has revealed the nature of her husband to her [Connie], dominant yet impotent, asserting his will over the machine, turning it into a moral support, blind to the fact that he is utterly dependent upon it, morally as well as physically."[5] Clifford's "dominant yet impotent" physical body resembles a machine and the surrounding industrial reality.

Both Connie and Mellors struggle against the insanity of the industrial world. When Connie arrives back at Wragby from a trip, she observes the colliery: the "mines had made the halls wealthy. Now they were blotting them out, as they had already blotted out the cottages. The industrial England blots out the agricultural England. [. . .] The continuity is not organic, but mechanical" (156). Later, the narrator describes Connie's thoughts: "Connie was absolutely afraid of the industrial masses. They seemed *so weird* to her. A life with utterly no beauty in it, no intuition, always 'in the pit'" (80). Mellors further denigrates industrialism as the fault of the world. After their first sexual encounter, he reflects:

> The fault lay there, out there, in those evil electric lights and dia-bolical rattlings of engines. There, in the world of the mechanical greedy, greedy mechanism and mechanized greed, sparkling with lights and gushing hot metal and roaring with traffic, there lay the vast evil thing, ready to destroy whatever did not conform. Soon it would destroy the wood, and the bluebells would spring no more. All vulnerable things must perish under the rolling and running of iron. (119)

Connie's fear of the mechanical colliery and Mellors's denunciation of industrial mechanism echo perfectly with Lawrence's well-known criticism of industry. Connie's and Mellors's resistance against the insanity of the modern world is also Lawrence's struggle with the degenerated civilization. In his essay "The Novel and the Feelings," he contemplates the degenerated insanity:

> But supposing they [horses] were left still shut up in their fields, paddocks, corrals, stables, what would they do? They would go insane.
> And that is precisely man's predicament. He is tamed. There are no untamed to give the command and the direction. Yet he is shut up within all his barb-wire fences. He can only go insane, degenerate.[6]

Lawrence personifies himself in Connie and Mellors to declare his sentiments repeatedly.

Industrial civilization also renders people money driven, greedy, and detached from each other. The most conspicuous separateness among people is the chasm between men and women—the unhealthy heterosexual relations. Lawrence delineates Clifford's thought about the "bitch-goddess" of success, which has two appetites. One appetite is "for meat and bones" which "were provided by the men who made money in industry" (107). Vehemently repudiating the appetite for money, Mellors further points out the growing fissure between man and woman:

> Look at yourselves! That's workin' for money! [. . .] You've been workin' for money! Look at Tevershall! It's horrible. That's because it was built while you was working for money. Look at your girls! They don't care about you, you don't care about them. It's because you've spent your time working and caring for money. You can't talk nor move nor live, you can't properly be with a woman. You're not alive. Look at yourselves! (220)

Lawrence reveals the problems that are intertwined: industry, money, and unhealthy love. Mellors actually repeats Lawrence's deep concern about the disconnection. In his essay "Men Must Work and Women as Well," Lawrence claims that "we see the trend of our civilization, in terms of human feeling and human relation. It is, and there is no denying it, towards a greater and greater abstraction from the physical, towards a further and further physical separateness between men and women, and between individual and individual."[7]

Connie's and Mellors's thoughts and claims critique Clifford's world harshly. Their adulterous love and their final union not only further deconstruct the order of the industrial society but more importantly constitute a new order composed with tenderness and life. In *The Virgin and the Gipsy*, Lawrence revolts against the social order by presenting sexual love as a pure opposition. In *Lady Chatterley's Lover*, he goes further by providing a solution, the deep communication of sex in the couple's own world, which also serves as the antithesis to Clifford's rationality, industry, and money-driven world.[8] Sexual love is not limited to being merely the defiant desire that questions the existing social order, as it is in *The Virgin and the Gipsy*. Connie's and Mellors's adulterous love provides the first step toward an organic new life. This love generates organic, natural, new life after betraying the sick marriage that represents modern falsehood.

The world made up of man and woman is the fortress that resists the modern sickness, represented by Clifford and Wragby. Connie and Mellors regard each other as an indispensable haven in the insanity of the world. Connie meditates to herself when she discovers the catastrophe of industrial Wragby: she "felt there was no next. She wanted to hide her head in the sand: or at least, in the bosom of a living man. The world so complicated and weird and gruesome! The common people were so many, and really, so terrible" (159). She believes that men and women need each other as allies to resist modern insanity and regain their lives in their own world of love. Despairing over the lifeless Wragby, Connie is desperately driven to escape into Mellors's love.

In turn, Mellors, a veteran who has witnessed the death of war and the madness of the modern world, at first recoils in isolation, but eventually he achieves a tender connection to Connie. He offers the solution when he and Connie discuss the wreck of the world: "'It's the courage of your own tenderness'" (277). "Tenderness," the original title of *Lady Chatterley's Lover*, is a key concept in this fiction.[9] Out of compassion, Mellors takes Connie and rebuilds the tie to the world even though that means "a new cycle of pain and doom" (119). In that scene, Connie cries for the waste of her womanhood at the sight of the little bird from the coop. When Mellors sees her tears, he is "aware of the old flame shooting and leaping up in his loins. [. . .] There was something so mute and forlorn in her, compassion flamed in his bowels for her" (115). It is this tenderness of compassion that ignites the couple's flame of love.

For Lawrence, the tenderness of love is compassion, the primordial blood relation to others. Lawrence proposed a new form of relationship when he wrote a letter to Witter Bynner on March 13, 1928: "The leader-cum-follower relationship is a bore. And the new relationship will be some sort of tenderness, sensitive, between men and men and men and women."[10] Accordingly, Connie's and Mellors's love embodies Lawrence's definition of love.

Adulterous love, detached from the civilized world, creates life on the mechanical industrial wasteland. For Lawrence, love is life, and life is closely associated with nature. Lawrence explicitly discloses the life Connie and Mellors create and share when they make love in the forest. "The man [Mellors] heard it beneath him with a kind of awe, as his life sprang out into her" (134). Connie also deeply senses this force of life in her womb after she returns to the room from the rendezvous. "It feels like a child in me," she feels. "So it did, as if her womb, that had always been shut, had opened and filled with a new life, almost a burden, yet lovely" (135). Life here indicates more than the child conceived in Connie's womb. Life, embodied in the primordial sexual connection, is a mysterious force that is opposed to deathly intellectualism and mechanical industry. Lawrence attempts to establish a new religion that worships primordial, natural, and organic life. Through primitive physical connection, people can resurrect their primal selves and recreate a new world. This adulterous love not only defies the modern discourse, as sexual love does, but more importantly complicates the defiance by offering a generative alternative to modern existence. Adultery takes on this role because it is opposed to all existing social forms. The transgression that it embodies is far from just a personal one. It becomes for Lawrence the beginning of a broader social transformation that promises to undermine and dissolve the existing order of human relationships.

This vision of an alternative order, full of life and organic connection, is always far from civilization but close to nature. Lawrence links the adulterous love to organic and primordial living force by setting the sex scenes in the world of nature. The countryside, filled with prehistoric living force, metaphorically opposed to the Wragby colliery, is beyond modern insanity. As John Humma maintains, "In *Lady Chatterley's Lover* the turbulent outer ring is, of course, the modern mechanistic society epitomized by Clifford Chatterley's collieries; the pastoral circle is Wragby Wood; the sacred center is the pheasant hut."[11] Indeed, Connie perceives the "unspeaking reticence of the old trees" in the wood as the "potency of silence" (65). The Wragby Wood symbolizes life as opposed to the deathly industrial collieries. Connie and Mellors create their own world through sex in the wood, where the flower of love grows in "the tree of Life."[12] After spending the night with Mellors in his hut, Connie stands "in the little front garden, looking at the dewy flowers, the grey bed of pinks in bud already." She tells Mellors, "'I would like to have all the rest of the world disappear [. . .] and live with you here.'" Lawrence then writes, "They went almost in silence through the lovely dewy wood. But they were together in a world of their own" (213).

For Lawrence, this world is dynamic, filled with organic and natural life. In the flower-decorating scene, the naked couple remains close to the earth and nature by marrying each other in flowers. Mellors "brought columbines and campions, and new-mown-hay, and oak-tufts and honeysuckle in small bud. He fastened fluffy young oak-sprays round her head, and honeysuckle withes round her breasts, sticking in tufts of bluebells and campion: and in her navel he poised a pink campion flower, and in her maidenhair were forget-me-nots and wood-ruff" (228). After Connie "pushed a campion flower in his moustache, where it stuck, dangling under his nose [Mellors declares that] 'this is John Thomas marryin' Lady Jane'"

(228). The imitation of a wedding in this flower scene pushes the novel to a triumphant climax that exalts their adulterous love: a celebration of an organic and natural life through the primordial union of man and woman. Adulterous love, even if sinning and transgressive in the modern social order, is pure, fulfilling, vigorous, and ideal in the natural order. This love in nature creates a utopia where connection and life become possible.

Connie's and Mellors's love in nature complies with Lawrence's concept about love and life. In "A Propos of 'Lady Chatterley's Lover,'" Lawrence exclaims:

> Oh, what a catastrophe for man when he cut himself off from the rhythm of the year, from his unison with the sun and the earth. [. . .] We are bleeding at the roots, because we are cut off from the earth and sun and stars, and love is a grinning mockery, because, poor blossom, we plucked it from its stem on the tree of Life, and expected it to keep on blooming in our civilized vase on the table.[13]

Love, as one's most evident existence, should remain rooted in the "tree of Life," rather than being uprooted and placed in the "civilized vase." Unshackling themselves from the civilized, industrial, and mechanical society around them, Connie and Mellors resurrect their life through love's unison with "the sun," "the earth," and "the tree of Life." Connie's and Mellors's organic love filled with life demonstrates and repeats Lawrence's declarations about love and life.

Symbolic and metaphorical, Lawrence's characters and scenes embody his own criticism and philosophy. *Lady Chatterley's Lover* is a dialogue between what Lawrence argues for and what he argues against. Colin Clark observes, "On the one hand the violent and metallic and mechanical and on the other hand growth and tenderness and sex. And these steep contrasts are sustained for the greater part of the novel."[14] Kingsley Widmer also draws our attention to Lawrence's critical sense of "desire/ negation dialectics," which encompasses "the green utopianism of the pastoral to negate modern society."[15] This dualism permeates the whole fiction. The ending, with the victorious consummation of adulterous love, is Lawrence's solution to the modern insanity of an industrial wasteland. Although many people consider his vision naive and idealistic, Lawrence's representation of an adulterous love that is warm, tender, and organic provides a solution to what he sees as a deathly, modern degeneration.

The Chinese Wife Caged in Decadent Desolation

Writing almost half a century later, Eileen Chang practiced her own aesthetics of desolation in another story of adultery. Different from Lawrence,
Chang denies the possibility of true love, the most intimate interpersonal
relation in "The Golden Cangue." With no such solution as tender love,
she projects a bleak picture of desolate Chinese modernity through a
failed adulterous love. A negative utopia surfaces from a contrast between
golden moments of true love and long-lasting desolate reality. After the
attempts at adultery are denied, the glittering moments of envisioned love
are devoured by moments of desolation and an ensuing destruction. In
"The Golden Cangue," Qiqiao's hope is destroyed by her husband and her
husband's brother Jize, whom she loves. In her despair, Qiqiao encounters
the moment of desolation and then proceeds to devastate herself and the
people close to her. By the end of the story, she has ruined the happiness
of her children. With her life wasted and consumed, Qiqiao is a victim to
a loveless dystopia but later bizarrely transforms into a tyrant who inflicts
sufferings upon her own children.

We may connect the private psychology of a suppressed woman to the
overarching public psychology in twentieth-century China. Qiqiao's story
represents a reaction against modernity in early twentieth-century China, a
period of rapid transformation as China entered the modern world. Qiqiao's
life is as ruinous as the radical changes inflicted on China during its modern
transition. But where Qiqiao is unaware of larger social issues, Chang herself
imparts a feeling of deep anxiety and desolation in her story. The discourse
of modernization in China revolves around a series of sociopolitical revolutions that embrace Western ideas and ways of life, including individual
freedom to love and marry. One striking example is the tremendous popularity of Ibsen's Nora after *A Doll's House* was translated and received in early
twentieth-century China. Following this model of a strong woman who
resolutely leaves her husband and children for a new life, Chinese readers
and writers believed that individual freedom of choice in love is the means
to emancipate women and to further debunk obsolete Chinese culture. Traditional ideas and culture were quickly dissolving in the age of revolution
when everyone welcomed radical transformations. Different from most of
her peers who steadfastly worshipped modernization, Chang was conserva-
tive in the face of radical changes and destructions, although she clearly saw
the downside of Confucian convention.

Ibsen's Nora reminds us of Lawrence's Connie, who also unconventionally leaves her marriage and her old life. However, Nora simply leaves everything behind without attempting to change or destroy what exists before. She also never develops any love relation outside marriage, therefore bringing less damaging force than Connie or even Chang's Qiqiao. Instead of creating a Nora figure in her story, Chang locks the wife to a "golden cangue" for us to pause longer and ponder upon the way in which Chinese modernity is caught between the traditional and the modern. Like Lawrence, Chang believed that the dominant form of modernization stands upon a base of traditional norms and order, establishing thereby a continuity in traditional structures of economy, ideology, and love relations. Skeptical with regard to both tradition and modernity, Chang lingers longer in the transition period by staying at the crossroad, with the weapon of adulterous love in her hand, to destroy the old structure that is now also the base of China's modernity. However, the existing structure is too tight to be destroyed, just as the domestic space is too claustrophobic to breathe. Opposing the blind optimism that her peers held toward modernization, Chang was pessimistic, anxious, and even fearful of the imminent and ongoing revolution.

The destruction and desolation in this story, therefore, can be juxtaposed with the relics left by modernization, constantly reminding us of the rapid transformation that leads to such anxiety. Writing as China was moving into a period of turmoil during World War II, Chang nonetheless transmutes this sense of anxiety and desolation into a form of literary aesthetics that she calls "de-cadence," or an intentional contrast between a past of hope and a future of despair. Instead of resorting to the perfect reunion between men and women, as Lawrence did, she tells a story of broken relationships.

For Chang, desolation is displayed through the de-cadenced contrast (*cenci de duizhao* 參差的對照). In "Writing of One's Own," she uses this term, which here is translated "equivocal contrast":

I like tragedy and, even better, desolation. Heroism has strength but no beauty and thus seems to lack humanity. Tragedy, however, resembles the matching of bright red with deep green, an intense and unequivocal contrast. And yet it is more exciting than truly revelatory. The reason desolation resonates far more profoundly is that it resembles the conjunction of scallion green with peach red, creating an equivocal contrast. I like writing by way of *equivocal contrast* because it is relatively true to life.

我是喜歡悲壯，更喜歡蒼涼。壯烈只有力，沒有美，似乎缺少人性。悲壯則如大紅大綠的配色，是一種強烈的對照。但它的刺激性還是大於啟發性。蒼涼之所以有更深長的回味，就因為它像蔥綠配桃紅，是一種參差的對照。我喜歡參差的對照的寫法，因為它是較近事實的。[16]

Chang adopts this equivocal (de-cadenced) contrast to reflect the truth of life—the desolation of the modern time. When talking about her concept, she contrasts it with Western tragedy, which she understands in terms of strength, not merely unhappiness. Her desolation is not strong but depressing and equivocal. As she explains in "On Writing,"

It is good if one can burst into tears. However, the sadness I write about is how you feel when you see a basin of dirty clothes. [. . .] The odor of the dirty clothes [. . .] the uncleanness and messiness choke one's sadness.

若能夠痛痛快快哭一場，倒又好了，無奈我所寫的悲哀往往是屬於「如匪澣衣」的一種。[. . . . . .]堆在盆邊的髒衣服的氣味[. . . . . .] 那種雜亂不潔的，壅塞的憂傷。[17]

Ostensibly, Chang renders salient the dark side of human nature, like the odor of dirty clothes. C. T. Hsia translates her concept as "impersonal sorrow over the perversity and pettiness of all passions" and indicates how Chang internalizes it in gynocentric monologues.[18] For Chang, as I argue here, this sadness is intimately linked to the darkness and the unpleasantness that contrast with the ephemeral moment of true love.

Love, the brightest facet of human nature, is repetitively denied and negated in Chang's work. Yet, it is the absolute denial of love in the lives of the female characters that renders love meaningful and significant, as necessary as the sun. Chang's characters gradually retreat into darkness. For example, Chang symbolically describes Qiqiao's daughter, Chang'an 長安, withdrawing into the sunless upstairs because of Qiqiao's malicious deeds:

Ch'ang-an [Chang'an] came downstairs quietly, her embroidered black slippers and white silk stockings pausing in the dim yellow sunlight on the stairs. After stopping a while she went up again, one step after another, to where there was no light.

長安悄悄的走下樓來，玄色花繡鞋與白絲襪停留在日色昏黃的樓梯上。停了一會，又上去了，一級一級，走進沒有光的所在。[19]

Just as Chang'an withdraws into darkness, her mother, Qiqiao, transforms herself into a calculating, spiteful, and pernicious creature living in the dark. Chang's sense of desolation reaches its climax when Qiqiao's loveless and dark nature contrasts with bright moments of love. Jize rejects Qiqiao, and then she in turn destroys her daughter's happiness and her son Changbai's marriage. Qiqiao's cruelty culminates in desolation.

The protagonists, Qiqiao, Jize, Chang'an, and Changbai, are unlovable because they are selfish, calculating, and loveless. Chang pushes to the extreme what one might otherwise understand as the effects of Confucian patriarchy. As a victim of the bleak society, Qiqiao suffers further degrees of agony and even becomes evil herself. The logic of Confucian patriarchy echoes the utilitarian, pragmatic logic of modernization. The idea of love was either meticulously constrained to support Confucianism or enslaved to serve the nationalist cause in modern China. Chang explores the woman's private thoughts to reveal a public psychology that is suffocating, violent, and dark. Qiqiao is a complex character who has a genuine longing for love, but her inability to love destroys her genuineness and pushes her into darkness. Her desire for love and her genuine feeling bring out the destructiveness in her nature.

Chang exposes this destructive darkness in the second half of Qiqiao's life, after her love is frustrated. Her madness, multilayered and complicated, develops gradually and slowly, accompanied by suffering and agony. As she remains in a loveless marriage, her madness and evilness become more evident and devastating. When the love she offers to Jize outside of her marriage is frustrated, she becomes paranoid, shifting her hysteria from the imagined lover to her money. She worries that her relatives will steal her money or that her daughter will marry her cousin as a way to get at her money. Chang adds the concerns about money to emphasize the connection between Qiqiao's desolation and a wasteland filled with fragmented relics.

For Chang, it is characters like Qiqiao's husband and Jize, who have no love in their heart or mind, that represent a wasteland of emotions. Their coldness contrasts with the warmth of Lawrence's Mellors. Qiqiao's husband barely talks to her or pays sexual attention to her. Jize defrauds Qiqiao by confessing his fake love. Love does not exist among these selfish and despicable people. Living with her invalid husband, Qiqiao is frustrated by the loveless marriage. She reveals her loneliness and bitterness when she flirts with Jize: "'Go sit next to your Second Brother. Go sit next to your Second Brother.' [. . .] 'Have you touched his flesh? It's soft and heavy, feels like your feet when they get numb . . .'"[20] She craves love that is full of life and freshness. Confined to the unfortunate marriage, she connects her husband's lifeless flesh to the dead flesh that is sold by her suitor Chaolu:

> Ch'ao-lu [Chaolu] plucked a piece of raw fat a foot wide off the hook and threw it down hard on the block, a warm odor rushing to her face, the smell of sticky dead flesh . . . She frowned. On the bed lay her husband, that lifeless body . . .

> 朝祿從鉤子上摘下尺來寬的一片生豬油,重重的向肉案一拋,一陣溫風撲到她臉上,膩滯的死去的肉體的氣味......她皺緊了眉毛。床上睡著的她的丈夫,那沒有生命的肉體......[21]

Similar to Lawrence, Chang uses the physical disability to symbolize the fatal flaw in the relationship between husband and wife. Qiqiao detests her disabled husband, and she so longs for other men's sexual attention that she seems bitter, even morbid. But men are incapable of mutual love. Qiqiao's marriage, her first failed heterosexual relation, is followed by the adulterous longing for Jize. She tells Jize about her miserable marriage life. Even though Qiqiao cries as hard as Connie does in *Lady Chatterley's Lover*, Jize, unlike Mellors, denies her love, and Qiqiao falls deeper into the dark:

> She slid down from the chair and squatted on the floor, weeping inaudibly with her face pillowed on her sleeve; the diamond's flame shone the solid knot of pink silk thread binding a little bunch of hair at the heart of the bun. Her back convulsed as it sank lower and lower. She seemed to be not so much weeping as vomiting, churning and pumping out her bowels.

> 她順著椅子溜下去,蹲在地上,臉枕著袖子,聽不見她哭,只看見髮髻上插的風涼針,針頭上的一粒鑽石的光,閃閃掣動著。髮髻的心子裏縶著一小截粉紅絲線,反映在金剛鑽微紅的光焰裏。她的背影一挫一挫,俯伏下去。她不像在哭,簡直像在翻腸攪胃地嘔吐。[22]

Her inaudible weeping, like the diamond's flame, expresses her love long-ing. At the end of the flirtation, Qiqiao stares "straight ahead, the small, solid gold pendants of her earrings like two brass nails nailing her to the door, a butterfly specimen in a glass box, bright-colored and desolate."[23] Trapped and distorted in the deathlike marriage, she is as beautiful and desolate as the butterfly specimen.

Jize, unlike Mellors, is unable to project his compassion onto the woman who bursts out in tears. In contrast to Mellors, whose "compas-sion flamed in his bowels for her" (115), Jize shuns this potential scandal. Merely concerned about himself, he pragmatically chooses not to take any risk. Looking at Qiqiao weeping, Jize wonders about himself:

> He loved to play around but had made up his mind long ago not to flirt with members of the family. When the mood had passed one would neither avoid them nor kick them aside, they would be a burden all the time. Besides, Ch'i-ch'iao [Qiqiao] was so outspoken and hot-tempered, how could the thing be kept secret? [. . .] Why should a young man like him take the risk?

> 玩儘管玩，他早抱定了宗旨不惹自己家裏人，一時的興致過去了，躲也躲不掉，踢也踢不開，成天在面前，是個累贅。何況七巧的嘴這樣敞，脾氣這樣躁，如何瞞得了人？[. . . . . .] 他可是年紀輕輕的，憑什麼要冒那個險？[24]

In his mind, there is no concept of compassion, let alone love. A woman is merely something he can use and abandon.

In Jize, Chang thoroughly depicts the shadowy psychology of a selfish and hypocritical man. Physically and emotionally deformed in this story, men are unable to provide real love for Qiqiao. This sort of unhealthy heterosexual relation cannot breed the fruit of love. Chang's equivocal or de-cadenced contrast between Jize's shallow, calculating personality and Qiqiao's genuineness (when she confesses her suffering) results in the sense of desolation Chang seeks to represent.

In Chang's view, once love is denied, the destructiveness of a dark human nature enters the center stage. Unfulfilled in a loveless life, Qiq-iao gradually sinks into madness and evilness. Her madness emerges and grows during her lifeless marriage with her suffocating, invalid husband. Qiqiao's sister-in-law observes her slight lunacy after she pays her a visit several years after Qiqiao's wedding. "'How is it this *ku-nai-nai* of ours has changed so? Before she was married she may have been a bit proud and talked a little too much. Even later, when we went to see her, she had more of a temper but there was still a limit. She was not silly as she is now, sane enough one minute and the next minute off again, and altogether disagreeable.'"[25] Each time that Jize quenches the flame of her love, it is followed by Qiqiao's increased insanity and destruction, leading to the sense of desolation. The first time is when she confesses her loneliness, yet Jize rejects her because he fears a scandal. The second occasion takes place after her husband dies and Qiqiao inherits the share of his family's property.

With the hope to rely emotionally on the closest man, Qiqiao generates and develops a special affection toward Jize, who is robust and attractive. Yet Jize attempts to swindle her by feigning his love for her. He confesses that he loves her, and Qiqiao, a woman desiring love, is deeply touched. Here Chang presents the reader with one of the rare moments when Qiqiao is lovely and likable. Chang sets up the de-cadenced contrast by presenting a beautiful thought in an otherwise unlovable person's mind:

> [Qiqiao] bowed her head, basking in glory, in the soft music of his voice and the delicate pleasure of this occasion. So many years now, she had been playing hide-and-seek with him and never could get close, and there had still been a day like this in store for her. True, half a lifetime had gone by—the flower-years of her youth. Life is so devious and unreasonable. Why had she married into the Chiang family? For money? No, for meeting Chi-tse [Jize], because it was fated that she should be in love with him.

> 七巧低著頭，沐浴在光輝裏，細細的音樂，細細的喜悅......
> 這些年了，她跟他捉迷藏似的，只是近不得身，原來還有今天！
> 可不是，這半輩子已經完了——花一般的年紀已經過去了。人
> 生就是這樣的錯綜復雜，不講理。當初她為什麼嫁到姜家來？
> 為了錢麼？不是的，為了要遇見季澤，為了命中注定她要和季
> 澤相愛。[26]

Shrewd, vulgar, and monstrous, Qiqiao is not at all an amiable and lovable character in this story, yet in this passage Chang gives her this beautiful and innocent thought.

For Chang, love, no matter whether it is merely a fantasy or not, inspires sincerity and goodness and transforms a woman into a woman in love. Qiqiao becomes an equivocal person, cruel and mischievous but also pitiful and genuine. No matter how mad and pernicious she is, there is a soft spot in her heart. This de-cadenced contrast between the aesthetic moment when Qiqiao is in love and the darkness of the rest of her life creates an artistic sense of desolation.

To achieve the sense of desolation in her stories, Chang masterfully depicts characters who have a conflicting nature. On the one hand, Chang reveals how wicked and pernicious people can be. This darkness of human nature is usually intentionally avoided and overlooked by Chinese writers. On the other hand, Chang romanticizes "the ordinary," in Ou-fan Lee's words, and discloses the fleeting but shining thoughts of these common people.[27] Desolation remains tinged by a glittering beauty that shines from darkness. The beautiful moment serves as a foil to the darkness of human nature. The paranoia, insanity, and villainy in Qiqiao's later life contrast with the moments of her imagined utopian love.

Once Qiqiao sees through Jize's conspiracy, she chooses money over insincere love. In the same scene, Qiqiao suddenly throws her fan at Jize and desperately tries to hit him. Jize indicates to the servants that she is crazy and asks them to send for a doctor. Jize then leaves, and the story leaves readers to feel the lingering sense of desolation. We feel how the previous beautiful moment of love is contrasted with the present cruel reality. Chang represents this feeling by describing how sour plum juice trickles down the table that Jize hits: "Drop by drop, the sour plum juice trickled down the table, keeping time like a water clock at night—one drip, another drip—the first watch of the night, the second watch—one year, a hundred years. So long, this silent moment."[28] This moment of empty silence represents an eternity of desolation.

Chang further represents desolation as the pursuit of money, the only human activity possible in Qiqiao's loveless world. Her sexual passion rejected, Qiqiao dramatically exhibits an inhumanity that destroys herself and the people close to her. Extremely paranoid about her money, she pursues wealth to such an extent that she compels her relatives to part from her and hate her. She insanely suspects them of swindling her, as Jize had done. Always seeking to control things, she becomes extremely possessive of her two children—Changbai and Chang'an—as she confines and ruins their lives and marriages. To prevent Chang'an from choosing her own husband, Qiqiao binds her feet no matter how much it hurts. When Chang'an grows up and falls in love with Tong Shifang 童世舫, an eligible man newly returned from Germany, Qiqiao interferes when she sees her daughter quit smoking opium and become a better lady:

Ch'ang-an [Chang'an] brought back some of the stray dreams under the starlight and became unusually silent, often smiling. Ch'i-ch'iao [Qiqiao] saw the change and could not help getting angry and sarcastic. "[. . .] Now you've got your wish and are going to spring out of the Chiangs' door. But no matter how happy you are, don't show it on your face so much—it's simply sickening."

長安帶了點星光下的亂夢回家來，人變得異常沈默了。時時微笑著。七巧見了，不由得有氣，便冷言冷語道：「[. . . . . .] 這下子跳出了姜家的門，稱了心願了，再快活些，可也別這麼擺在臉上呀——叫人寒心！」[29]

To sunder the attachment between Chang'an and Shifang, Qiqiao invites him to have dinner behind Chang'an's back and strategically indicates to him that Chang'an smokes opium and that the Jiangs (the family of Chang'an's father) are decadent and corrupt. Shifang is shocked and leaves Chang'an forever. Qiqiao's monstrous mania is depicted through Shifang's eyes. When he sees Qiqiao at the dinner, he "instinctively felt this was a mad person. For no reason there was a chill in all his hairs and bones."[30]

Qiqiao's lunacy is embodied in her unreasonable attitude towards her daughter's happiness. She is both jealous of the happy daughter and afraid of losing her, for a daughter is precious property to a family. In the darkness of Qiqiao's villainy, however, shines the beauty of Chang'an's desolated feelings when Shifang leaves her. Knowing Shifang will not see her again, "Ch'ang-an [Chang'an] quietly followed behind, watching him out."[31] The suppressed sadness echoes with the fragile beauty of the "light yellow daisies on her navy blue long-sleeved gown."[32] Chang'an's feeling of desolation is closely linked to the delicate beauty of Chang's notion of decadenced contrast (*cenci de duizhao* 參差的對照).

The equivocal, absurd, and complicated Qiqiao and the other unlovable characters in a loveless world exhibit to the reader a hopeless existence of desolation. Yet the desolation is artistically aesthetic to Chang. The phrase "beautiful, desolate gesture" appears twice in the story, which is sufficient to demonstrate Chang's sense of desolation through the decadenced contrast in this story.[33] The contrast between the inevitable, eternal desolation and the rare utopian love moments reveals Chang's anxious perception of a Chinese modernity that is always forward looking and cruelly optimistic.

Adulterous Love and Women's Power

Lawrence and Chang are both aware of a deep chasm between men and women in modern society and observe that the heterosexual relation is rarely mutual and reciprocal. They then affirm the validity of adulterous love as a means to empower women so as to transgress against the existing order in each of their societies. On the one hand, the idea of adulterous love elevates women and empowers them with autonomy and freedom. On the other hand, women's power determines the fulfillment of adulterous love. Here, women's power is a form of gender power that can attract men's attention, so that they can have an equal and mutual communication. Although subversively critiquing modern existence in each of their societies through adulterous love, Lawrence and Chang formulate this transgressive love distinctively. The writer's optimistic or pessimistic attitude toward women's power determines the mode of adulterous love.

Lawrence presents an invincible love between an aristocratic wife and a working-class veteran who together regenerate warmth, connection, and life in a Western industrial wasteland. Connie's power suffices to excite her lover's compassion for her, and she eventually achieves a successful adulterous love. Consequently, the lovers are able to recognize each other through compassion and sexuality, thereby bonding communally to create life and bonds in an open space of nature.

Different from the optimistic Lawrence, Chang pessimistically believes in the impossibility of an equal and mutual heterosexual relationship, and the adulterous relation is never fulfilled in Chang. The lack of love between men and women results in the frustration of women's power. Qiqiao's husband, using his power of wealth, deprives her of her sexuality and her subjectivity. The unloved wife breeds children but later brings them up to be living dead in a claustrophobic domestic space.

Jize, devoid of any notion about love and women's sexuality, is also unable to recognize Qiqiao's gender power, which relies on men's recognition of her subjectivity and sexuality. Left without the experience of mutual recognition, she does not experience the successful adultery that Connie lives, and Qiqiao's gender power remains confined and suppressed. She attempts to empower herself through wealth, but she still fails to reconcile with her opposite sex through sexuality and love. The failed husband-wife relation and the failed adultery demonstrate a deformed heterosexual relation; that is, man and woman are unable to live in unison physically and emotionally when women's gender power is unrecognized and undermined. The potential lovers, trapped in their family money and selfish logic of utilitarianism, are unable to recognize each other and love, and they are thereby carried along their one-way psychological path. There is an unbridged chasm between man and woman in the story where women's sexuality and emotional needs are denied and effaced. Women, isolated and overlooked by men, can only project their own voices without men's echo and response. The result is a woman's one-sided monologue that tells a story of desolation.

The chasm between man and woman in Chang's work can be interpreted allegorically as the opposition of a masculinist discourse of nationalism and utilitarianism against the feminine discourse of gender and women's subjectivity in the process of China's modernization.[34] Unlike Lawrence, whose major discourse in *Lady Chatterley's Lover* is dialectic, Chang's narration always dwells on the women's perspective, which is, in Wendy Larson's words, "overwhelmingly feminine, destructive, and uncontained."[35] Chang's gynocentric perspective, opposed to Lawrence's androgynous insight, demonstrates the deformity and non-communicativity of heterosexual relations in both the private and the public spheres.

Dystopian Vision of Modernity in Lawrence and Chang

The contrast between the victorious adulterous love in the West and the failed one in China can conveniently lead to such banal conclusions as "the West is much more open than China" or "women have more autonomy in the West." If Lawrence's novel were realistic and Chang's were impersonal, then the comparison would naturally lead to these conclusions. However, in *Lady Chatterley's Lover*, Lawrence infuses his fiction with social-political thinking and utopian optimism; therefore, the novel is more metaphorical and symbolic than realistic. Likewise, Chang's story is more an expression of her literary aesthetics than a realistic recording of Chinese society; therefore, it is heavily encoded and emblematic. Chang also insists upon the aesthetics of desolation in which beauty and tragedy are intertwined through de-cadenced contrast. In other words, the "truth" revealed in her story is tremendously colored with her own aesthetics and the cultural critiques behind it. Many scholars believe that this story reveals the way in which Confucian conventions suppress women's subjectivity. Another interpretation of Chang's solipsistic authorial view toward modern reality is that the domestic reality in this story reflects Chang's countercultural response to China's early period of modernization.

Therefore, the remarkable contrast of the two endings of the stories demonstrates the two authors' distinctive responses toward the same discourse of modernization. Lawrence and Chang determine the endings of their stories and the fate of their characters. Lawrence argues against the cold rationality, mechanism, and industrialism personified by Clifford. By contrast, Mellors and Connie represent warm body, organic life, and nature. The two parties form a dialectical argument in Lawrence's fiction. Lawrence eventually allows Mellors and Connie to triumph over Clifford. Their final choice to sunder the tie to society is their thorough declaration of anarchy, which is Lawrence's main political stance. The happy ending is not realistic but symbolic, carrying Lawrence's assertive worldview and his sincere hope for utopia on earth. The adulterous love manifests Lawrence's response to social flaws in the dominant modern discourse. Man and woman can achieve real life and establish a new world through deep and primeval sex. This adulterous love defined by sexual union heals the fissure not only between man and woman but also between earth and heaven. The triumph of adulterous love provides an antidote to modern isolation and religious collapse.

Chang's sense of desolation is deeply rooted in her reaction to Chinese modernity and her own anxiety about her career. In "On the Second Edition of Romance," she expresses her anxiety to publish her stories and become successful: "Hurry! Hurry! Otherwise it will be too late! Too late!"[36] She is also extremely anxious because she constantly feels threatened by the destructive transformation of modern China. As she elaborates: "Even if I were able to wait, the times rush impatiently forward—already in the midst of destruction, with a still-greater destruction yet to come. There will come a day when our civilization, whether sublime or frivolous, will be a thing of the past. If the word I use the most in my writing is 'desolation,' that is because this troubling premonition underlies all my thinking."[37]

Although Chang writes only about domestic affairs, not politics, China quickly transformed from a stable Confucian society toward a Western-ized, modern China during the historical period in which she lived. Traditional philosophy and Confucianism had collapsed in the middle of the nineteenth century when modern Western countries, such as Great Britain, France, and Germany, invaded and colonized China. In 1912, the last imperial dynasty, the Qing dynasty, was overthrown and replaced by the

Republicans. In 1919, nationalism officially entered the center of the socio-political and cultural agenda. Western thought and nationalism replaced Confucianism. China underwent a dramatic revolution not only in politics but also in culture and ideology. "The Golden Cangue" expresses Chang's anxiety in such a historical crisis.

Believing that desolation reveals the truth of the age, Chang created a world replete with darkness, insanity, and sadness. Rather than fighting heroically as Lawrence did, Chang applied her aesthetics of desolation by digging into the darkness of human nature in a society where love and sexuality could be utilized and traded.[38] Love, the most essential element in human life, is debased as a practical means to gain quick money or social advancement in this story. The failure of the adulterous love between Qiqiao and Jize demonstrates Chang's pessimistic conviction that love is impossible, even though the freedom to choose one's partner was highly promoted and practiced by other Chinese modernists.

For Chang, sadness rather than strength is the carrier of aesthetic value. Therefore, she directs her literary interest toward disillusion and darkness, engendering a profound sense of desolation. In "Writing of One's Own," Chang explicitly elaborates her aesthetic theory:

> I find that, in many works, strength predominates over beauty. Strength is jubilant and beauty is mournful. [. . .] "Life and death are so far apart / I make my vow to you / and take your hand / to grow old together." This is a mournful poem, but how very affirmative is its posture toward human life. I do not like heroics. I like tragedy and, even better, desolation. Heroism has strength but no beauty and thus seems to lack humanity.

> 我發覺許多作品裏力的成分大於美的成分。力是快樂的，美卻是悲哀的 [. . . . .]「死生契闊，與子成說；執子之手，與子偕老」 是一首悲哀的詩，然而它的人生態度又是何等肯定。我不喜歡壯烈。我是喜歡悲壯，更喜歡蒼涼。壯烈只有力，沒有美，似乎缺少人性。[39]

Chang elaborates her signature aesthetic view in this important observation. Beauty is defined by desolation because it reveals the deep reality of human existence. Chang upholds desolation and sadness as the form of beauty, thereby foregrounding the darkness of human existence and the impossibility of love. Chang's desolation is expressed through a mournful illustration of life, and her emphasis on the desolation of human existence explains why she dwells on love and human relations in her works.

Further, cold desolation, like *yin* 陰, the opposite of *yang* 陽, is featured with femininity and extreme emotion. Ou-fan Lee insists, "If the power and glory of war and revolution are manifestly masculine, then the aesthetic state of sorrowful desolation is certainly feminine."[40] Rey Chow further theorizes Chang's femininity in her idea of "feminine detail." Sensuous details that are emotionally contextualized are released in literature to offer an alternative modernity and history. To elaborate this idea, Chow uses Chang's negative feelings in "The Golden Cangue" as a case study. Chow recognizes the "problems of femininity" as "the central focus in the fictional writings of Eileen Chang, in which an alternative approach to modernity and history arises through a release of sensual details whose emotional backdrop is often that of entrapment, destruction, and desolation."[41] In contrast to Lawrence's dialectical discourse, Chang persists in a gynocentric monologue in "The Golden Cangue." Her literary subject is Qiqiao's desolation, particularly her desire, desperation, madness, and evilness, which stem from her profound sense of isolation and loneliness.

Literary aesthetics seem irrelevant to politics. However, as the next chapter further elaborates, Chang's aesthetic theory of desolation is a demonstration of Theodor Adorno's negative utopia. If Chang insists on desolation as the essential aspect of beauty, it is because it is only with the backdrop of desolation that one can arrive at a longing for the utopian. With the utopian moment, art projects an alternative to desolation that merges a private with a public vision. Art and political intervention converge at the moment of utopia, which stands out within a larger context of desolation.

Lawrence's symbolic reality and Chang's desolation are their artistic attempts to reveal the weaknesses of modernity in order to find other modes of existence. Both authors offered vehicles to another dimension of the modern world: Lawrence's man-woman world and Chang's aesthetic world of desolation. Lawrence wrestles with the darkness and tries to bring hope and solution. Even though he emphasizes mechanism and death, Lawrence creates triumphant plots and characters because he believes in strength, eventually offering a myth of paradise in the secular world. For Lawrence, woman and man have their gender powers, but no one wins over the other. Lawrence reconciled the two genders through tenderness in the deep communication between woman and man. Love is generated and developed in the fulfillment of their sexuality. After exposing the defects and sickness in heterosexual relations, Lawrence provides the solution—the warm, deep communication of sex. The success of adulterous love in *Lady Chatterley's Lover* embodies Lawrence's heroic courage, the courage to resist tragedy and create a new world upon the wasteland. As he writes in the beginning of the novel, "We've got to live, no matter how many skies have fallen" (1). In contrast to Lawrence's persistent heroic claim, Chang sets her story in the dark color of desolation. In the beginning of the story, she writes that "the best of moons is apt to be tinged with sadness."[42] Adulterous love is doomed in Chang's world, because she obliquely accepts, even highlights, an aesthetics of desolation that is driven by a bleak vision for Chinese modernity: the impossibility of love, a dark human nature, and revolutionary destruction. The aesthetics adopted by Lawrence and Chang differ in their approach to tragedy. Lawrence's aesthetics is determined by his binary beliefs: strength versus weakness, victory versus failure. His worshipping of strength and triumph reminds us of the tragic Greek hero who demonstrates unyielding will and power and dies for glory and victory. Embracing heroism in Greek tradition, Lawrence unequivocally declares an affirmative utopia by fighting against the dark and the bad. His aesthetics, embodied with his philosophy, is his way to engage with the sociopolitical problems. In contrast, Chang limits her aesthetic project to exploration and definition of what beauty is in literature and art. The beauty she believes in and attempts to create is not Lawrence's strength and triumph of a hero. Rather, beauty to her is another kind of tragedy that is more related to Chinese tradition than the Western one, a tradition that recognizes but passively accepts a world with desolation and darkness. Instead of trying to fight the desolate world, as Lawrence does, Chang accepts such a dark reality but at the same time seeks and savors the very rare portion of utopian moments of love in her writings. For Chang, the glittering moments of love, no matter how buried and suppressed, will emerge and create a utopia against the major background of darkness and desolation. This is the beauty she believes in and attempts to create. Her aesthetics of de-cadenced contrast embodies this very essence of her philosophy.

FOUR

The Twin Utopias of Transcendental Love

After defying both local and global discourses to reach a cosmopolitan freedom, Lawrence and Chang discovered that freedom lies not necessarily somewhere outside but inside a heart that longs for an alternative utopian existence. The longing for utopia develops into an increasingly stronger theme in their later writings, displaying their redemptive attempts to create a new language of God's love. In Lawrence's and Chang's semiautobiographical novels, *Women in Love* (1920) and *Xiao tuanyuan* 小團圓 (*The Little Reunion*, 2009),[1] the search for self-fulfillment leads to self-transcendence. In both novels the main characters start out isolated and are then given ways to move beyond modern society. Lawrence, a priest of love, seeks an alternative secular transcendence through an individual vitalism that replaces the collapsing collective religion in the West. Likewise, Chang, a pessimistic idealist, persistently seeks a personal response to the fall of Buddhist tradition in Chinese high culture.

Both Lawrence and Chang believe love, essentially a relation, transfers lovers to another mysterious dimension of utopia. The transcendence that love can breed is intimately connected to the depth of time and the cosmos. With the global collapse of religious beliefs, both authors reflect upon life and the universe profoundly and metaphysically in order to replace the eroded religious tradition in each of their own cultures. Attempting to break restrictions in their local cultural discourse, Lawrence attains his secular rebirth through primitive sexual union, while Chang's understanding of transcendence wavers between a "golden eternity"[2] and Buddhist disillusionment.

Scholars frequently approach Lawrence's *Women in Love* from a metaphysical perspective, including critics such as Sarah Urang, P. T. Whelan, and John Humma.[3] Harold Bloom affirms Lawrence's spirituality by starting the introduction to his book *D. H. Lawrence's Women in Love*:

"Lawrence, hardly a libertine, had the radically Protestant sensibility of Milton, Shelley, Browning, Hardy—none of them Eliotic favorites. To say that Lawrence was more a Puritan than Milton is only to state what is now finely obvious."[4] Lawrence's focus on sexuality is in fact paradoxically puritan and provides the basis for his transcendental love.

To establish a basis for transcendence in love, *Women in Love* focuses primarily on two couples' relations. Rupert Birkin loves and clashes with Ursula Brangwen. Gerald Crich—a wealthy industrialist—has an affair with Ursula's sister, Gudrun Brangwen, whom he seeks out to find comfort from his tortured, inner destructive force. Yet, Gudrun remains independent and defiant; and her rejection of Gerald leads to his suicide in the Alps. The disastrous relation between Gerald and Gudrun is juxtaposed with the fulfilling love between Birkin and Ursula, whose thoughts and remarks are modeled on the relationship between Lawrence and his wife, Frieda. Unlike Gerald, Birkin achieves a sacred resurrection in his sexual union with Ursula. As a sequel to *The Rainbow*, *Women in Love* continues the metaphysical search for an overarching heaven that is eventually obtained on earth.

In contrast to those of Lawrence, scholars of Chang have barely probed the metaphysical aspect of *The Little Reunion*, whose transcendental orientation actually permeates the structure of the novel. Most of the primary studies on *The Little Reunion* focus on its context and form rather than its content. Clara Iwasaki uses *The Little Reunion* as one example among Chang's autobiographical novels to detail its creation, publication, circulation, and reception in an autobiographical context.[5] Revolving around the integration of autobiography and fiction in Chang's later works, Deborah Tze-lan Sang argues that *The Little Reunion* demonstrates "a unique and precious marriage between imagination and factuality."[6] Attempting to unpack Chang's late style with Edward Said's ideas, Jiwei Xiao dwells on Chang's personal frustration as a lover, daughter, and writer rather than on her poetic self.[7] However, a closer look at this poetic self that is entrapped and displaced in the larger geopolitical context of postcolonialism in both Sinophone China and the United States reveals a metaphysical dynamic that is embodied in the aesthetics of negative utopia.

The Little Reunion recounts Sheng Jiuli's 盛九莉 life, starting with her college years in Hong Kong, her frustrated desire for parental love, and her first love with Shao Zhiyong 邵之雍 in Shanghai, with constant flashbacks to her childhood, her youth, and her abortion after she relocates to the United States. It is commonly noticed that the love between Jiuli and Zhiyong in *The Little Reunion* is based on Chang's first love and informal marriage to Hu Lancheng 胡蘭成. Jiuli, a lonely and sensitive girl, is in love with Zhiyong, a national traitor and unfaithful lover (someone who will remind us of Mr. Yi in "Lust, Caution"). Chang relives the prime time of her life through writing and revising this semi-autobiography in order to make sense of countless jumbled and garbled pieces of banal reality, which stand in contrast to the rare moments of golden eternity. Like Birkin, she delivers herself to the dimension of eternity through the experience of earthly love. But where for Lawrence transcendence is a vibrant, potent, sexual renewal, Chang's transcendence is scattered in brief moments of utopia that are eternalized through the aesthetic gaze of looking back.

Lawrence's Transcendental Love on Earth

Relationships serve as the key to secular transcendence in both stories. It is the longing for oneness that drives characters to establish a connection with another. Aristophanes defines love in Plato's *Symposium* as mankind's desire for oneness:

> Everybody would regard it [the desire to be together] as the precise expression of the desire which he had long felt but had been unable to formulate, that he should melt into his beloved, and that henceforth they should be one being instead of two. The reason is that this was our primitive condition when we were wholes, and love is simply the name for the desire and pursuit of the whole.[8]

If love is a "desire and pursuit of the whole," it is inherently metaphysical and carries a strong sense of longing for transcendence. Through love, human beings can retrieve the lost half of their selves, and the totality will lead to the ultimate transcendence. Birkin explicitly delivers this understanding of the relationship when he and Ursula are discussing marriage and the bond between man and woman. "I do think," Birkin remarks, "that the world is only held together by the mystic conjunction, the ultimate unison between people—a bond. And the immediate bond is between man and woman."[9] For Lawrence, the intimate relation between man and woman is the essential form of a person's relation with the cosmos.

Lawrence's conception of the cosmos starts at the beginning of time.

In the chapter "Excurse," after expressing their mutual love, Birkin and Ursula "drifted through the mild, late afternoon, in a beautiful motion that was smiling and transcendent" (311). Their sexual ritual, profoundly connected to a mythical, prehistoric primitiveness, facilitates the lovers' return to the origin of time, the beginning of the world, as God's descendants.[10] While caressing and making love with Birkin, from "a strange reality of his being, the very stuff of being, there in the straight downflow of the thighs," Ursula sees Birkin as "one of the sons of God such as were in the beginning of the world, not a man, something other, something more. [. . .] It was the daughters of men coming back to the Sons of God, the strange inhuman Sons of God who are in the beginning" (313). One page earlier, when they hear a hymn played by Southwell Minster bells, Ursula feels a transcendental moment that overtakes her in their sexual consummation. "This was no actual world, it was the dream-world of one's childhood—a great circumscribed reminiscence. The world had become unreal. She herself was a strange, transcendent reality" (312). The feelings of transcendence precede the lovemaking scene near the cathedral. Such images as "sons of God who are in the beginning" and "the dream-world of one's childhood" are intertwined with their sexual union when Birkin and Ursula deliver themselves to the beginning of the world. The sexual reunion, temporally mythical and spatially utopian, is a process of redemption that reconnects the lovers to the origin of being. By negating time, the lovers turn themselves into the children of God. Lawrence repeatedly emphasizes this primitiveness in the novel and in his philosophical works.

Lawrence believes that sex, the bridge to the past, transfers the characters out of their current civilized life and into the ancient root. As Birkin claims to Hermione, a former lover who believes in mind, primitive instinct is better than a deathly, civilized mind: "Better be animals, mere animals with no mind at all, than this, this *nothingness*" (41). Birkin later describes instinctual "sensuality" as "'the great dark knowledge you can't have in your head—the dark involuntary being.' [. . .] 'In the blood [. . .] when the mind and the known world is drowned in darkness.—Everything must go—there must be the deluge. Then you find yourself a palpable body of darkness'" (41). Lawrence considers this dark knowledge, or blood-consciousness, as the meaning of making love. As he writes in one of his essays, "Sleep and Dreams": "Sex is our deepest form of consciousness. It is utterly non-ideal, non-mental. It is pure blood-consciousness. [. . .] The blood-consciousness is the first and last knowledge of the living soul: the depths."[11] He attempts to reach the depths, the distant origin, through the ritual of "primal desire," as Birkin explains this impulse (146).

Lawrence also transfers the lovers Birkin and Ursula to an asocial space free from their society and close to a new existence. In "Excurse," while having dinner at the cathedral, Birkin expresses his wish to live somewhere unfettered by social rules. "There's somewhere where we can be free—somewhere where one needn't wear much clothes—none even [. . .] where you be yourself, without bothering" (316). In the chapter "A Chair," when they see the furniture in the street, Birkin again claims his ideal: "You must leave your surroundings sketchy, unfinished, so that you are never contained, never confined, never dominated from the outside" (356–57). Lawrence repeatedly expresses his ideal to live in another world free from society, asserting that two lovers can form a new "extraordinary world of liberty" (205). Birkin reveals the possibility of living in such a new world when Gerald inquiries about where his special world is. "'Make it.—Instead of chopping yourself down to fit the world, chop the world down to fit yourself.—As a matter of fact, two exceptional people make another world. [. . .] Do you *want* to be normal or ordinary?—It's a lie. You want to be free and extraordinary, in an extraordinary world of liberty'" (205). This extraordinary world of liberty is created by two lovers who are isolated from the extraneous, mechanical society.

Lawrence's developing philosophy of sex and love lies behind Birkin's meditation about love on the day before the marriage. It suggests a transcendent love beyond the social sphere:

It [love] was not the real truth. It was something beyond love, such a gladness of having surpassed oneself, of having transcended the old existence. How could he say "I", when he was something new and unknown, not himself at all? This I, this old formula of the ego, was a dead letter.

In the new, superfine bliss, a peace superseding knowledge, there was no I and you, there was only the third, unrealised wonder, the wonder of existing not as oneself, but in a consummation of my being and of her being in a new One, a new, paradisal unit regained from the duality. (369)

Through earthly love Birkin acquires "the real truth," "the new, superfine bliss, a peace superseding knowledge." Birkin finds love "in a consummation of my being and of her being in a new one, a new, paradisal unit." He concludes that it "transcended the old existence." Feeling reborn, Birkin continues his pondering, "How can I say 'I love you', when I have ceased to be, and you have ceased to be, we are both caught up and transcended into a new oneness where everything is silent, because there is nothing to answer, all is perfect and at one" (369). Speech is irrelevant because his love excludes the mundane world. Silence indicates an unknown paradise. The oneness in sex puts Birkin in direct touch with the mysterious cosmos and the vast universe.

In "A Propos of 'Lady Chatterley's Lover'" Lawrence elucidates the existential transcendence that is so important in *Women in Love*. Phallus, a significant symbol in Lawrence's world, serves as "the connecting link" to the "oneness" he experiences as the "highest achievement of time or eternity":

> [The] phallus is the connecting link between the two rivers [of man and woman], that establishes the two streams in a oneness, and gives out of their duality a single circuit, forever. And this, this oneness gradually accomplished throughout a life-time in twoness, is the highest achievement of time or eternity.[12]

The intimate interrelation between the two lovers forms the bridge between humanity and the Absolute. He inherits the ideologies of numerous Western philosophers, primarily Arthur Schopenhauer and Friedrich Nietzsche.[13] Simultaneously, he assimilates and appropriates Christianity, Buddhism, and Taoism to create an alternative secular practice of transcendence at the turn of the twentieth century when old beliefs were being questioned and dissolved.[14]

Secular Redemption of Realities in Lawrence

At the turn of the twentieth century, theosophy, transcendentalism, and literature were tempered by Eastern religions. The prevalence of theosophy, transcendentalism, and Eastern religions demonstrates the attenuation of Christianity in Western society. It was an era of transition filled with changes and crisis, during which Lawrence attempted to create a new religion. William Y. Tindall observes that this time was

> a place where machines have suddenly multiplied the population and elevated a class without what Mr. Eliot likes to call sensibility. The popular education decreed by this class has at once spread

knowledge and spread it thin. The sudden concentration of people in cities has killed the local roots which nourish sentiments. And what seems worse, science and materialism have destroyed for many writers the religious traditions upon which their feelings once centered and their art.[15]

It was a civilization that worshipped materiality and became alien to spiritual pursuits. Discontented with this culture and seeking cures for themselves and the world, some artists, like Lawrence, attempted to rediscover and invent a spiritual substitute for the faith they had lost. For Lawrence, this transcendental experience, primarily erotic and sexual because he identified sexual consummation as the act of love, takes the form of ultimate mystical union. "In the act of love [. . .] Man is with God and of God."[16] Sex is "the deepest of all communions, as all the religions, *in practice*, know. And it is one of the greatest mysteries: in fact, the greatest, as almost every apocalypse shows, showing the supreme achievement of the mystic marriage."[17] The numinous experience of the union with the sacred realm of being is happening in the present and simultaneously beyond the earthly world.

Lawrence wrote to a friend in 1912 from Lake Garda in Italy, "I shall always be a priest of love, and a glad one. Once you've known what love can do, there's no disappointment and no despair."[18] As the priest of love, he uses phallus as the metaphor of his religion. The Lawrentian metaphor of phallus reminds us of Jacques Lacan's theory, which links this modern writer to a postmodern discussion. Hilary Simpson was the first to briefly recognize this affinity between Lawrence and Lacan, indicating that "Lawrence occasionally uses the symbol of the phallus in a similar way."[19] It will be interesting to examine whether Lacan was inspired by Lawrence, who pointed out the significant signifier of phallus. Lacan asserts:

> The phallus is the privileged signifier of this mark in which the role [*part*] of Logos is wedded to the advent of desire.
>
> One could say that this signifier is chosen as the most salient of what can be grasped in sexual intercourse [*copulation*] as real, as well as the most symbolic, in the literal (typographical) sense of the term, since it is equivalent in intercourse to the (logical) copula.[20]

Also, Lacan comments in *Speech and Language in Psychoanalysis*, "The phallus is not a question of form, or of an image, or of a phantasy, but rather of a signifier, the signifier of desire. In Greek antiquity the phallus is not represented by an organ but by an insignia; it is the ultimate significative [sic] object, which appears when all the veils are lifted."[21]

For Lawrence, as for Lacan later, the phallus serves as the central signifier of the fulfillment of human desire. Ursula in *Women in Love*, for example, "had thought there was no source deeper than the phallic source. And now, behold, from the smitten rock of the man's body, from the strange marvelous flanks and thighs, deeper, further in mystery than the phallic source, came the floods of ineffable darkness and ineffable riches" (314). Lawrence's biblical diction (e.g., "smitten rock," "floods") demonstrates his attempt to elevate the phallus to the transcendental representation of fulfillment, as his narrator explains in *Lady Chatterley's Lover*:

> It is prior to the personality. And the personality must yield before the priority and the mysterious root-knowledge of the penis, or the phallus. For this is the difference between the two: the penis is a mere member of the physiological body. But the phallus, in the old sense, has roots, the deepest roots of all, in the soul and the greater consciousness of man, and it is through the phallic roots that inspiration enters the soul.[22]

Preceding Lacan's representational sense of the phallus, Lawrence crystalizes a secular transcendence through "the deepest roots" of "the phallus."

Lawrence's recognition of the "phallic roots" suggests that he was aware of phallic cults in various religions, such as those the modern scholar John Allegro describes. More importantly for Lawrence, however, the phallus represents the essence of his private religion, which centers on the interrelation to others as well as on experience through sexual feeling, the culmination of the union.[23] The more completely and profoundly the lovers are sexually connected, the more sacred and transcendental their passionate love becomes. Through sexual union, lovers achieve the ultimate, mystical marriage in order to fulfill their unknown desire. Francis Kunkel praises Lawrence's heroic devotion to the "unconventional but sincere religious faith" that is closely engaged with sex. Kunkel argues, "[Lawrence] repeatedly pointed out, the one sure way to make sex filthy and sensual beauty degrading is to to separate them from mysticism and spiritual beauty. The Lawrentian hero, the man who died, embraces the truths of the body and uses them as the basis of an unconventional but sincere religious faith."[24] Lawrence's last novel, *The Escaped Cock* (or *The Man Who Died*, which is Lawrence's preferred title, 1929), represents his last attempt to find redemption by replacing Christianity with a secular practice of healing and rebirth.

Even though Lawrence worships this transcendental existence, the mysterious unknown actually dwells on the earth, between man and woman, in the enigma of sexual marriage. Charles Burack observes, "The felt recognition of the aliveness of the cosmos and of one's fundamental connection to it constitutes the essence of sacred experience."[25] The connection, symbolized by the phallus, is embodied in the sacred experience on earth. Lawrence brings the unknown living force down to mundane life and relates earthly experience to a transcendental existence.

Negative Utopia in Eileen Chang

If Lawrence's transcendence is achieved through the optimistic recreation of God's love, Eileen Chang, by contrast, sublates earthly love into a utopian domain that opposes itself to an utterly negative reality. Chang scatters brief but significant moments of the golden eternity of love in *The Little Reunion*, whose primary ground is otherwise based on bleakness and suffering. Chang's transcendence is fulfilled through negative utopia, in Adorno's sense of a longing for utopia amid hopeless sufferings, not utopia itself. In his *Aesthetic Theory*, Adorno elaborates the crucial relation between utopia and negation: "Only by virtue of the absolute negativity of collapse does art enunciate the unspeakable utopia."[26] The "collapse" echoes with darkness and suffering in Chang's historical and private realities. For Adorno, the "real possibility of utopia . . . converges with the possibility of total catastrophe."[27] For Chang, the possible moment of utopia converges with a primary time of desolation and disillusion. In contrast to the negation and collapse of the external, the internal moment of utopia exists for Adorno in the "briefest of spaces," "a fleeting scene, not as a place of lingering."[28] Chang's utopian transcendence is composed with very brief, fleeting moments of love that are set against a heavy desolation and darkness. Also, the transcendental moments in the aforementioned stories "The Heart Sutra," "Lust, Caution," and "The Golden Cangue" further demonstrate her idiosyncratic means of utopian transcendence.

Compared to scarce and brief moments of utopian transcendence that occupy remarkably little space in *The Little Reunion*, most of the novel recounts the disparaging and painful experiences of Jiuli's childhood, youth, and adulthood. Chang spent half of her life remembering her early life in China after migrating to the United States. Among a series of her autobiographical novels, *The Little Reunion* starts with the middle point of her life when she was thirty years old and jumps around before or after this point of time to primarily remember her college years in Hong Kong and her childhood and youth in Shanghai. Like the old Proust, who was trapped by disease and poverty, Chang, living in diaspora and oblivion, was seeking consolation from her youth, even though desolation, suffering, and trauma abound during the best of her years.

The novel starts and also ends with the same paragraph that strikes an extremely bleak note as a motif to remind us of life's inevitable experience of pending horror. "In the morning of final exam, the dismal mood can only be felt by troops in dawn before battle, like rebel slave troops in *Spartacus* peering through dawn mist at the Roman armies, which is the most horrific scene among war films, because of the pure waiting."[29] After two paragraphs, Chang writes that one of the benefits of getting old is no more exams, "yet [Jiuli] still had dreams about taking final exams, always nightmares."[30] Horror and anxiety about imminent misfortune prevail throughout the rest of the novel. The extreme lack of parental love, the catastrophe of World War II, the failed love relationships, and countless disparaging but disappointing incidents in her life all weigh "like a heavy tombstone pressing on her heart."[31] Most of the time, Jiuli's suffering renders her detached and seemingly insensitive, just like Chang herself.

This strong sense of emptiness and disillusionment forms part of a longer tradition shared by traditional Chinese literati.[32] However, Chang makes a crucial move to counter this aesthetic and metaphysical tradition by believing in the possibility of a utopian transcendence that follows upon disillusionment.

Desolation and Disillusionment in Chang

Composed of twelve chapters, *The Little Reunion* details a woman's fragmented remembrance of countless trivial incidents, subtle interpersonal relationships, and her inner response to all the disappointments in her life. The responses are always unpleasant, disappointing, and negative because of her unrequited love. Her mother left for foreign countries when Jiuli was a child due to the unhappy marriage with her father. Jiuli, only a child, precociously sees through life's emptiness without much parental love, just like her first memorable taste of life: "a white copper spoon" with an unpleasant "fishy smell."[33] Her father violently beats and imprisons her after he remarries, while her mother always blames Jiuli for being a burden, especially financially. The mother-daughter relation is based on money rather than love, which renders Jiuli excessively obsessed with money. In order to return the money she owes to her mother, as well as to become financially independent, Jiuli studies hard in Hong Kong with the hope of study in England in the future. This explains her constant anxiety and fear of the final exams that directly determine her career and fate. In this sense, Jiuli shares the same destiny with her precursors: traditional Chinese literati whose fates were tightly linked to their success in imperial examinations. The novel starts with her Hong Kong time, when she is closest to emancipation from a loveless life and at the start of a hopeful new life in England. By gazing back, Chang realizes that the Hong Kong period was a turning point that defined the rest of her life. All the students' records are set on fire by the registrar because of the Japanese invasion in Hong Kong. Jiuli's only hope of embarking on a new life is thus denied in this moment when her individual pursuits for the first time intersect with social turbulence and the capriciousness of fate. When she joins the circle to see the fire, only one look is enough "to never forget about it as if it were imprinted in her heart. [. . .] The grade records are all burnt as if her approaching life-long achievements had floated away."[34] The moment of seeing all the grade records on fire, just like other moments of disillusionment, is briefly and lightly depicted but delivers a profound sense of disenchantment and melancholy. One of her rare chances to redeem herself from a loveless family life and to channel her passion into a career is also gone.

The lack of love from her mother's side, therefore, drives Jiuli to eagerly seek the warmth of love from other people's stories: her aunt, her cousins, her servants, her friends, her stepmother, even her husband, Shao Zhiyong. The hunger for love saturates her fragmented remembrances, providing a warm distraction from war, family conflicts, crisis, loneliness, and countless disillusions.

If the book is heavily marked with Jiuli's frustrated love with her mother, her inscrutable and helpless love for Zhiyong is equally important in leading to her later disenchantment. Traumatized by Zhiyong's multiple betrayals, Jiuli is disillusioned by man-woman love, even twenty years after she leaves Zhiyong.

In contrast to Lawrentian victorious transcendence in sex, Chang's primitive sex symbolizes an impalpable fear and an inarticulate pain stem-

ming from the loss of a child. Jiuli faces a wood-inscribed bird, "primitively sculptured," while Zhiyong is caressing her on a sofa.[35] Jiuli is disturbed and intimidated by the bird, and she doubts "whether the bird is a
primitive idol that her ancestors worshipped." "The bird is staring at her."[36]
This sex scene is mingled with a profound sense of crudeness and coldness because of the presence of the primitive horrific wood bird. In the
maternity hospital, "these things [sex and reproduction] are taboo to her.
She feels that sex and reproduction are passed down from the most primitive ancestors. Sex and reproduction are forms of mystery and horror
at the core of life."[37] Having doubly failed in both sex and reproduction,
Chang has an idea of sex that dramatically differs from Lawrence's notion
of interrelationship. With the repetition of the image of the wood bird,
this exact sex scene with her first husband in Shanghai is tightly linked to
the nightmarish abortion she undergoes twenty years after her migration
to the United States:

> At night under the bathroom light, she saw the male fetus in the toi-
> let. In her frightened eyes, it was ten inches long, standing between
> the white porcelain wall and water. Its flesh was covered with a faint
> layer of blood, like the light orange color of the newly polished
> wood. The blood congealed in its recesses clearly drew the fetus's
> outlines. A pair of disproportionately huge round eyes is protrud-
> ing and wings are tucked. It is the wood-inscribed bird at the door.

> 夜間她在浴室燈下看見抽水馬桶裏的男胎，在她驚恐的眼睛裏
> 足有十吋長，畢直的歆立在白磁壁上與水中，肌肉上抹上一層
> 淡淡的血水，成為新刨的木頭的淡橙色。凹處凝聚的鮮血勾劃
> 出它的輪廓來，線條分明，一雙環眼大得不合比例，雙睛突出，
> 挼著翅膀，是從前站在門頭上的木彫的鳥。[38]

The wood-inscribed bird, closely associated with traumatic intimacy,
holds a strong resemblance to the aborted fetus. This bizarre resemblance
reflects the unforgettable horror that has haunted the heroine. Reproduction, an act of creation, is depicted otherwise here. The ghastly sight of
the unborn child arouses intense feelings of wretchedness, repulsion, and
terror that are linked to her failed love with Zhiyong. Her disillusionment
over Zhiyong's love, just like this horrific flashback, recurs as a motif of
pain and desperation that accompanies Jiuli for the rest of her life. The
moment when she learns that Zhiyong has betrayed her for another young

girl in Wuhan, another gloomy moment when she discovers his unfaithfulness with another old woman in a village, and more such moments in which she experiences the sense of loss even decades after she immigrates to the United States all deepen and recall the miserable sense of disillusionment and emptiness she undergoes with her parents and her lover.

The inevitable emptiness and disillusionment revealed by Chang resemble the Buddhist insights that are embodied in traditional Chinese literature. *Jin Ping Mei* 金瓶梅 (*The Golden Lotus*, ca. 1600), a canonical Chinese novel, provides readers with religious enlightenment at the beginning:

> We may be so strong that, unaided, we can lift a cauldron or tow a ship, but, when the end draws near, our bones will lose their strength and our sinews their power. Though our wealth may give us mountains of bronze and valleys of gold, they will melt like snow when the last moment comes. Though our beauty outshine the moon, and the flowers dare not raise their heads to look on us, the day will come when we shall be naught but corruption, and men will hold their noses as they pass us by.[39]

The author advocates a Buddhist transcendence by unveiling the illusion and emptiness of the secular world. He quotes the famous line from one of the Buddhist classics, *Jin'gang jing* or *Chin Kang Ching* 金剛經 (*The Diamond Sutra*): "Well does the *Chin Kang Ching* speak of this foolish life 'as dream and as illusion; as lightning and as dew.'"[40] Here, life is denied as an empty dream.

The Buddhist emptiness is also manifested in another masterpiece, *The Dream of the Red Chamber*:

> Bleak haunts where weeds and willows scarcely thrive
> Were once with mirth and revelry alive.
> Whilst cobwebs shroud the mansion's gilded beams,
> The cottage casement with choice muslin gleams.
> Would you of perfumed elegance recite?
> Even as you speak, the raven locks turn white.
> Who yesterday her lord's bones laid in clay,
> On silken bridal-bed shall lie today.
> Coffers with gold and silver filled:
> Now, in a trice, a tramp by all reviled.

[. . .]
In such commotion does the world's theatre rage:
As each one leaves, another takes the stage.
In vain we roam.[41]

This famous novel, as one of the four greatest Chinese classics, delivers an equally deep sense of Buddhist disenchantment and sadness. In it, the author Cao Xueqin describes a predestined, tragic love between Jia Baoyu and Lin Daiyu. In chapter 1, a monk tells a Taoist about the axiom of Baoyu and Daiyu in their prelife when Baoyu was an unused stone. The fairy Disenchantment kept him in her palace and named him Divine Luminescent Stone-in-Waiting. He watered the beautiful Crimson Pearl Flower, the prelife Daiyu, and granted her with life. The dew the Stone watered enabled the Flower to "assume the form of a girl." "The consciousness that she owed the stone something for his kindness in watering her began to prey on her mind and ended by becoming an obsession." She believes that "the only way in which I could perhaps repay him would be with the tears shed during the whole of a mortal lifetime if he and I were ever to be reborn as humans in the world below."[42] Daiyu loved Baoyu with her tears in the Jia family after they both descended to the mortal world. Their love, a debt of tears, is mythically predestined to be doomed and tragic. Hence, the predestined love that Cao Xueqin narrates breeds a profound sense of disillusionment and emptiness. The novel contrasts a mighty force of mystery with people's powerlessness in order to demonstrate that any human effort is in vain and futile because everything on earth is merely illusion. Emptiness, the primary feature of Chang's love, similarly demonstrates a strong note of Buddhist nihilism. In fact, *The Golden Lotus* and *The Dream of the Red Chamber* are two traditional Chinese fictions that Chang immensely favored and closely studied. Undoubtedly, the Buddhist sense of emptiness and disillusionment had a profound impact on her.

Faced with a hopeless and frustrating life, the heroine Jiuli, Chang's fictional persona, chooses another type of transcendence that is closer to a Buddhist understanding about life and the cosmos, shared by traditional Chinese literati. Liu Zaifu, in his attempt to foreground Chang's sense of tragedy, affirms, "Chang is pessimistic about life, human civilization, and the world. To her everything in reality, things such as successes, failures, glories, and humiliations, will turn into nothingness and death in the end. So only nothingness and death are real."[43] Chang's disenchantment is expressed and embodied in her idiosyncratic aesthetics of tragedy. In this sense, Chang joins the traditional intellectuals' lamentations upon the tragedy of human existence and disillusionment.

Transcendental Utopia and Women in Love

Chang not only admits and accepts this Buddhist tradition, however, but more importantly transforms this inherently religious discourse into a secular practice of bringing heaven down to earth. In this regard, she resembles Lawrence insofar as they both redeem reality by creating an alternative secular practice of reformed religion. Chang complicates the question of tragedy by providing a negative utopia: a contradiction between utopia and desolation that does not seem to appear in the older Chinese literature. The very rare but crucial moments of utopia scattered in Jiuli's life, particularly when she is in love with Zhiyong, outshine the tragic desolation and disenchantment that pervade the rest of the novel.

In *The Little Reunion*, Chang presents a representation of transcendental love that is comparable with Lawrence's because they both achieve transcendence through utopian experience and feeling. At the early phase of romantic courting, Jiuli falls in love with Zhiyong. Jiuli pictures the utopia that she is experiencing:

> Time becomes long and boundless, like the golden desert, vast with nothingness but clarion music. Past and future are connected, which should be the eternity. Recently, life is so different, utterly isolated from other earthly affairs. She merely accompanies him on the path of life, rowing in the river of the golden dream, but she can get off the boat for the river bank anytime.

> 時間變得悠長，無窮無盡，是個金色的沙漠，浩浩蕩蕩一無所有，只有嘹亮的音樂，過去未來重門洞開，永生大概只能是這樣。這一段時間與生命裏無論什麼別的事都不一樣，因此與任何別的事都不相干。她不過陪他多走一段路。在金色夢的河上划船，隨時可以上岸。[44]

Chang unveils a transcendental existence through the experience of love. The woman in love experiences the golden eternity in the "golden desert." The transcendent moment experienced through love approximates a timeless and placeless eternity. Chang brings divine fulfillment down to mundane life and relates earthly experience to a transcendental utopia.

It is the amorous attachment that ultimately transcends the heroine, bringing her to the "golden river." Detached from earthly affairs, the golden eternity is the boundless nothingness in the "golden desert." Chang's golden eternity is similar to Lawrence's paradise filled with unknown truth, silence, and rebirth. Chang later explains that the transcendence is familiar to Jiuli for she "never felt so peaceful after her childhood was over."[45] She experienced this peaceful golden time in her childhood, just like the golden river described in the song that her mother and her aunt used to sing:

> Row the boat down to the river,
> The river of golden dream,
> Singing
> Love songs.

> 泛舟順流而下
> 金色的夢之河，
> 唱著個
> 戀歌。[46]

Jiuli recovers the paradisal and mysterious peace of her childhood, just as Lawrence discovers a mythical childhood through sex. Love, deeply related to childhood, is elevated and eternalized in the utopian past. Through love, Jiuli is reconnected to the golden time of her childhood, to a mythical past, and eventually to a golden eternity. The experience of love opens a gate to a temporal and spatial transcendence that sublates earthly existence.

Even though Zhiyong becomes unfaithful after their romantic relationship stabilizes, Jiuli, who utterly devotes herself to this romance, still experiences a utopian moment that counters the bleak reality. Jiuli's love poem reveals a love that is able to link to an ancient past and a mythical cosmos.

> I am not in his past.
> Lonely years are gone.
> Garden lies deep down.
> The empty room is covered with sunshine.
> It is already the ancient sun.
> I want to run in,

Shouting "I am here.
I am here!"

他的過去裏沒有我，
寂寂的流年，
深深的庭院，
空房裏晒著太陽，
已經是古代的太陽了。
我要一直跑進去，
大喊「我在這兒，
我在這兒呀!」[47]

Again, through love, Jiuli transfers herself to a timeless utopia, a garden covered with ancient sunshine, a place that reminds us of the aforementioned golden river, golden desert, and golden eternity.

Jiuli's desperate pining for her lover echoes Lawrence's emphasis on the relation with the Other. The Other constantly reminds us of our lack, our incompletion, and our mortality. The establishment of the relation with the Other facilitates Jiuli's desire to achieve self-transcendence. Lawrence's understanding of relation can illuminate the philosophy of Chang's desire to relate with the Other. He regards relation as "timeless and absolute" in his essay "The Crown." Lawrence claims in the same paragraph, "Behind me there is time stretching back forever, on to the unthinkable beginnings, infinitely. And this is eternity."[48] For Chang, the presence of love promises the existence of the timeless being and absolute actuality of utopia. Chang's mysterious ancient sunshine resembles Lawrence's attempt to return to the primal past through sexual union. The abandoned garden shining with the ancient sun is linked to the vastness of time and the depths of space. The mythical garden exists in the timeless nowhere, quietly detached from temporality. This love, as demonstrated by the mythical garden and the ancient sun, elevates Jiuli into a transcendent state of temporal and spatial limitlessness, just as Lawrence looks to sexual consummation to achieve immediate contact with the unknown mystery.

The Sense of an Ending

Both authors attempt to cross boundaries of human domain in time and space through the lived experience of love. They explore the transcendental dimension of utopia bridged by the extremity and intensity of love. Utopia, achieved through either Lawrence's sexual union or Chang's inscrutable love, carries a redemptive force that can generate alternatives to the bleak realities in each of their cultures. As Frank Kermode convincingly demonstrates, men "rush into the middest, *in medias res*, when they are born; they also die *in mediis rebus*, and to make sense of their span they need fictive concords with origins and ends, such as give meaning to lives and to poems. The End they imagine will reflect their irreducibly intermediary preoccupations."[49] Caught between the old and the new, Lawrence and Chang both live in the "middest" when Christianity had declined in the West and tradition was eroded in Chinese high culture. They make sense of their lives and fictions by relating them to origins and ends that are highly utopian and transcendental. The fictive endings project their visions about a distant future that echoes the beginning of human existence.

Yet, the structure of Lawrence's idea of utopia differs from Chang's. Lawrence optimistically believes that utopia can ultimately be achieved triumphantly, and he consequently always concludes his stories with consummation and revelation. For Chang, utopia is defined by its opposition, desolation and disenchantment. Hence, Chang's utopia is foregrounded with a tremendously negative, dark background.

From *Sons and Lovers*, *The Rainbow*, *Women in Love*, and *The Virgin and the Gipsy* to *The Escaped Cock*, Lawrence always ends with a hopeful note of victorious emancipation and fulfillment. The sense of an ending is not only mythically triumphant, as Kermode perceives, but also transcendentally utopian. Like Lawrence, Chang had always been pondering transcendental love metaphysically, thereby offering different patterns of fictive ending in her stories. The stories in her earlier writing career usually end with destruction, emptiness, and disillusionment, although love subversively transgresses and transcends the preexisting order.

In "The Heart Sutra," the father-daughter love is more than incest prohibition. Chang transforms Xiaohan into a mythical figure, living beyond the tangible mundane world. At the beginning of the story, Chang gives the readers a close-up of Xiaohan: "She had the face of a child in a fairy tale. [. . .] She had a strange, disturbing kind of beauty."[50] In the beginning of the story, Xiaohan is positioned between heaven and earth. Chang writes, "There wasn't anything else here, except the sky, Shanghai, and Xiaohan. No, the sky, Xiaohan, and Shanghai, since Xiaohan sat between the sky and Shanghai."[51] Sitting between the sky and the real world of

Shanghai, Xiaohan serves as a divine medium between heaven and the mundane world. Her love for her own father, thus, should not be interpreted as a merely disgraceful love affair or an Oedipus complex. Her love with a direct touch of the Absolute proves later to be a Buddhist lesson that invokes a sense of disenchantment.

The title "The Heart Sutra" echoes the sublime Buddhist classic of the same name that persuades people to stop pursuing illusion on earth. A famous line in the classic, "*Se ji shi kong, kong ji shi se*" 色即是空，空即是色, means anything material on earth is illusion.[52] Living is dying. Loving is collapsing, followed by the endless emptiness and silence. At the end of "The Heart Sutra," when Fengyi leaves his daughter Xiaohan for the daughter's friend Lingqing, Chang presents Xiaohan's love as something that is as scattered as her broken family.

> There they stood across the floor, across the mat in lemon-yellow and pearl-gray checks, across the cat which was fast asleep, the spittoon, the little patch of cigarette ashes, the scattered morning paper . . . her broken home! . . . It was only a short distance, yet it seemed to be filled with glass shards, sharp glass pieces. She couldn't hurry over to him. She couldn't get close to him.

> 在他們之間，　　隔著地板，　　隔著檸檬黃與珠灰方格子的地蓆，　　隔著睡熟的貍花貓、痰盂、小撮的煙灰、零亂的早上的報紙 . . . . . . 她的粉碎的家！. . . . . . 短短的距離，然而滿地似乎都是玻璃屑，尖利的玻璃片，她不能夠奔過去。她不能夠近他的身。[53]

Compared to the previous intimacy, the physical and emotional distance between Fengyi and Xiaohan in the end announces the end of their desire. This strong sense of emptiness and Buddhist transcendence annotates the story's title and persistently presents itself. Chang's early stories always end with desolation and emptiness, bringing readers Buddhist disenchantment.

Chang ends "Lust, Caution" and "The Golden Cangue" with grave destructions, silence, death, and disillusionment. Chang contrasts the eventual emptiness against illusions of earthly love. At the closure of "Lust, Caution," for example, "amid the raucous laughter, he [Mr. Yi] quietly slipped out."[54] The political conspiracy and the love affair, just like the "raucous laughter," are merely transient illusions on earth. Jiazhi's death and the silence Mr. Yi slips into at the end of the story signify an eventual sense of emptiness.

In "The Golden Cangue," after all the destruction she causes,

> Ch'i-ch'iao [Qiqiao] lay half asleep on the opium couch. For thirty years now she had worn a golden cangue. She had used its heavy edges to chop down several people; those that did not die were half killed. She knew that her son and daughter hated her to the death, that the relatives on her husband's side hated her, and that her own kinsfolk also hated her. She groped for the green jade bracelet on her wrist and slowly pushed it up her bony arm as thin as firewood until it reached the armpit.

> 七巧似睡非睡橫在煙鋪上。三十年來她戴著黃金的枷。她用那沈重的枷角劈殺了幾個人，沒死的也送了半條命。她知道她兒子女兒恨毒了她，她婆家的人恨她，她娘家的人恨她。她摸索著腕上的翠玉鐲子，徐徐將那鐲子順著骨瘦如柴的手臂往上推，一直推到腋下。[55]

Qiqiao, calculating and strong willed, achieves nothing but destruction and hatred during her entire life. She becomes the bony figure, consumed and bodily effaced by earthly banality and suffering. Her life turns out to be a futile ordeal, wasted in a golden cangue.

Chang maintains her aesthetics of Buddhist disenchantment in her later writings, including *The Little Reunion*, which, however, ends with Jiuli's sweet dream. Even though the sense of an ending differs from her early works in its presentation of a harmonious vision, this ending does not deliver a triumphant and reconciled state of a stable existence. Rather, it is merely another fleeting moment of utopia whose warmth, hope, life, and happiness will certainly be replaced by lasting desolation and bleakness:

> Once she had a dream with the background of *The Trail of the Lonesome Pine*, a film that she watched in childhood. [. . .] A reddish brown cabin on the green mountain, contrasted with the azure sky. Tree shadows are swaying. There are several kids in the pine forest. They are all hers. Here comes Zhiyong, smilingly dragging her to the cabin. Fairly funny, she suddenly turns bashful. At the moment

when their arms form a straight line she awakens. A film twenty years ago, a man ten years ago. She is happy for a long time after.

有一次夢見五彩片《寂寞的松林徑》的背景，身入其中，還是她小時候看的 [. . . . . .] 青山上紅棕色的小木屋，映著碧藍的天，陽光下滿地樹影搖晃著，有好幾個小孩在松林中出沒，都是她的。之雍出現了，微笑著把她往木屋裏拉。非常可笑，她忽然羞澀起來，兩人的手臂拉成一條直線，就在這時候醒了。二十年前的影片，十年前的人。她醒來快樂了很久很久。[56]

The supreme existence crystalized in the dream depicts the utopia that Jiuli craves. She encounters very briefly those utopian moments when she is in love with Zhiyong. Consequently, she has been longing for the feeling of utopia and quickly recognizes it when a similar utopian moment presents itself. Utopia for Chang cannot be engineered and structured to be made real, as the Marxist revolution or social democracy sought to do. It also differs from Lawrence's utopia, which presents itself as the culmination of a preceding development. Instead, Chang's utopia requires a constant gaze into the past while waiting to recognize those familiar utopian moments. The longing for utopia, not actualized or demystified, maintains the power of utopia as a redemptive force.

Living in the pine forests that are persistently green is a variant form of golden eternity. Children represent the vivacious living force and the everlasting love with her beloved. Only in this dream, she fulfills her ultimate goal in life and achieves redemption and rebirth despite the frustrations in reality that render Jiuli cynical, cold, detached, and pessimistic. As Chang herself claims in one of her letters, *The Little Reunion* "is a story of love and passion. I want to show love's vicissitude and its winding course. Even after this love is utterly disillusioned, there is still something left."[57] The remembrance of the utopia, something left from a deep experience of love, creates an eternal longing for the imminent utopian moments in the future. Contrasted with the desolate realities in the autobiography, the ending still promises, as Lawrence does, hopeful possibilities for utopia on earth.

In her essay "Love," Chang concisely presents an unnamed girl's unfortunate life in order to illustrate and answer the big questions: What is love? What is life? Readers can sense the cold desolation after reading about a young girl, as pretty as a peach blossom, as pure as moonlight, falling deeper and deeper into the morass of earthly life. Chang reveals at the end of the essay how love could be an unpredictable chance that generates utopia. She laments:

> When you meet the one among the millions, when amid millions of years, across the borderless waste of time, you happen to catch him or her, neither a step too early nor a step too late, what else is there to do except to ask softly: "So you're here, too?"[58]

> 於千萬人之中遇見你所遇見的人，於千萬年之中，時間的無涯的荒野裏，沒有早一步，也沒有晚一步，剛巧趕上了，那也沒有別的話可說，惟有輕輕的問一聲：「噢，你也在這裏嗎？」[59]

Set against a universe of vast desolation in time and space, one single chance for two people to meet and fall in love, for Chang, is rare, brief, but highly utopian. This contrast crystalizes with and echoes the negative utopia expressed and delivered in Chang's semiautobiographical fiction *The Little Reunion.*

Chang and Lawrence both long for a utopia that is mediated through a transcendental love. Living in an age of global faithlessness, both writers attempt to transcend themselves in the midst of earthly love in order to break the limitations of their local religious traditions. Lawrence does so actively and triumphantly, while Chang maintains and simultaneously critiques the preexisting Buddhist disenchantment by presenting love's paradox between rare moments of utopia and long-lasting sufferings, negatively evoking a sense of utopia in the contrast between the ephemeral moment of a golden eternity and a lifelong disillusionment.

Conclusion

The twentieth century was an age of revolution in which the secular gods of science, technology, nationalism, and modernization overthrew the old God. Today's scientific-technological advances in transportation and communication shorten distances between countries, bolstering a homogenizing modernization and secularization; but such progress simultaneously heightens contrasts and conflicts among cultures. In response to the century's secular modernism as well as clashes and uncertainties (world wars, cold war, terrorism, trade war, etc.), an old concept of a peaceful, unified world became an ever more alluring alternative to today's increasingly homogenizing but conflicted world. Cosmopolitanism, as put forward by political philosophers since Immanuel Kant, offers a vision of peace and freedom that can resist violent nationalism and hegemonic discourse. While this movement from ethnic conflict to "eternal peace" attempts to suppress nationalist inclinations in order to establish a cosmopolitan order, Lawrence and Chang, in contrast, develop a shared cosmopolitan project in which love as an ethical feeling plays a crucial role in creating cosmopolitan connections.

D. H. Lawrence and Eileen Chang both adopt love as their mode of engagement with the multidimensional world, from the local to the global to the universe. To Lawrence and Chang, love is a primal living force in its dynamic and undefinable state, which is tightly interconnected with utopia. It is utopia that fulfills the possibility of a jump from personal love to cosmopolitan engagement. Utopia should be understood as the longing for utopia, not the utopia itself. This longing takes four forms of love in Lawrence and Chang, driving art to disrupt the predominant orders on multiple levels. Starting with the incest prohibition, utopia for both writers is a free space that is a negative projection from out of their birth cultures' problems, just as both Xiaohan and Paul are overshadowed by their

117

parents' incestuous desires and eventually depart from their birth families for alternative heterosexual relationships. In the beginning, it seems that both writers seek their utopia by negating the deficiencies of their realities.

Yet, in moving to sexual love and adulterous love, the two writers develop more and more bifurcated utopian visions, affirmative and negative, to oppose dominant orders. The pending victory of the virgin and the gypsy is contrasted with the death of Jiazhi, whose desire for an alternative love relation is suffocated and suppressed. Lady Chatterley's thorough awakening and the lovers' final departure for a new life contrast with Qiqiao's rare and frustrating moments of an imagined love amid the lifelong imprisonment in her golden cangue. Lawrence triumphantly affirms a possible utopian existence, while Chang negates the bleak realities she presents by interweaving them with rare glittering moments of utopia.

The bifurcated vision of utopian engagement with the world becomes strongest and the most salient in transcendental love. Encapsulating their own worldviews, Lawrence and Chang inject a large dose of utopian revelation into their fictional egos, Birkin and Jiuli, to recreate an alternative faith through a new religion. Both writers are subjectively oriented by the vision of utopia, whether it is expressed positively or negatively.

Like Birkin and Jiuli, the writers spent half of their later lives beyond their local cultures in pursuit of a realm of utopia, geographically and subjectively. Lawrence embarked in 1919 on a time of voluntary worldwide exile, looking for his utopia beyond Britain. He found the possibility of utopia in nature while traveling and wrote the poetry collection *Birds, Beasts and Flowers* (1923). He implemented his utopian communist community at Taos, New Mexico, from 1922 to 1924. He also sought after the possibility of utopia in aboriginal and Eastern culture and wrote such exotic works as *Aaron's Rod* (1922), *Kangaroo* (1923), and *The Plumed Serpent* (1926). Yet, after all the attempts and experiments, Lawrence still ends his search for utopia in the realm of love. The Man, known as the resurrected Jesus in Lawrence's last novel, *The Escaped Cock*, is healed and regenerated through his sexual union with the priestess of the Isis in Search. The "marvelous piercing transcendence of desire" eradicates "the darkness in his soul," replacing it with "the deep, interfolded warmth" of a woman.[1] The restoration of a dying Man and the subsequent pregnancy of the priestess demonstrate a utopia that can be fulfilled through transcendental love. The novel also leads to a hopeful and optimistic vision for the future: "Tomorrow is another day."[2]

While Lawrence positively affirms, in an age of war, modernization, and religious decline, the possibility of an alternative utopian existence, Chang painfully looks back into bleak realities in order to retrieve her fleeting utopia in precious moments of love. Like Lawrence, she spent the second half of her life as a migrant writer in the United States shortly after the establishment of New China. Different from that of Lawrence, Chang's search for utopia is not spatial but temporal in her later career. For her, utopia lies in the moments of love, including the love for the past.

She had reacted pessimistically to a highly politicized social environment in both China and the United States. In the United States, Chang continued her passivity, detaching herself from the outer world either to (re)interpret her previous life back in China through literary creation or to immerse herself in translations of classical Chinese literary pieces, such as *The Sing-Song Girls of Shanghai* and *Dream of the Red Mansion*.[3] She also reflected upon her own life, translated her own works, and wrote the autobiographical novels *The Little Reunion*, *The Fall of the Pagoda*, and *The Book of Change*. During her struggle with Cold War policy and Orientalism in the United States, Chang fell back to the sentiment that she formulated in 1944: "We seek the help of an ancient memory, the memory of a humanity that has lived through every era, a memory clearer and closer to our hearts than anything we might see gazing far into the future. And this gives rise to a strange apprehension about the reality surrounding us," as she wrote in "Writing of One's Own."[4] She dissolved her sense of displacement through memory and nostalgia.

In their intense engagement with the theme of love, Lawrence and Chang inevitably lay out a broader vision of love's meaning for life. As Plato writes in the *Symposium*, love must ultimately be defined as the "desire for the perpetual possession of the good."[5] Love is far more than a personal affair and in fact essential to the very notion of a universal good. In China, two thousand years later, Tang Xianzu, the author of *The Peony Pavilion*, wrote, "Love is of source unknown, yet it grows ever deeper. The living may die of it, by its power the dead live again."[6] Like Plato, Tang Xianzu interprets love as the pathway to the deeper and broader meaning of humanity. Love creates life. As they explore love, Lawrence and Chang thus embrace this intense, profound feeling, push the limits of our humanity, and create a utopian structure of order. Utopia is not a geographical place on earth. Rather, it takes different forms in an ideal subject's heart. It first and foremost lies inside, not outside, because utopia is discovered and constructed by the authorial attempt to use love to engage with the world and eventually to transcend limitations to achieve freedom.

The analysis of love expands both vertically into higher levels of social order and horizontally toward different cultures. Vertically, starting from their own local cultures, Lawrence and Chang transgress their local conventions and traditions, then move up to oppose the discourses of nationalism and modernization on national and global levels, and eventually elevate love as a means to achieve an alternative utopia religiously and metaphysically. The vertical, expanding movement to engage socially in a larger world is juxtaposed with the progression of an ideal subject through parental, sexual, adulterous, and transcendental love. Horizontally, love in Lawrence and Chang and the two different cultures behind them form disparate linkages. Placing love at center stage in the world, both writers, with distinctive aesthetics and philosophies, adopt love as a means of navigating sociopolitical discourses toward alternative utopian visions in the twentieth century. The cosmopolitan love Lawrence and Chang develop in their writings redefines love, utopia, and cosmopolitanism to propose a new relationship among the three seemingly unconnected topics.

Utopia, for both Lawrence and Chang, serves as the crucial nexus that links love in the private sphere to a wider landscape of cosmopolitan engagement in the public sphere. Utopia, like the idea of cosmopolitanism, intrinsically carries a strong sense of sociopolitical function, thereby freeing the power of love from private concerns in order to engage with public ones. Adorno uses utopia as the standard to define what art is in relation to society. He observes, "Art must be and wants to be utopia, and the more utopia is blocked by the real functional order, the more this is true; yet at the same time art may not be utopia in order not to betray it by providing semblance and consolation."[7] The utopian visions instilled in the ideas of love in both writers shed light not only on the artistic features but more importantly on what is internal to art: sociopolitical critique of "the real functional order," in other words, the intervention into hegemonic discourses. This interconnectedness of art and utopia, therefore, renders the cosmopolitan love developed by Lawrence and Chang extremely political and socially significant.

For Chang and Lawrence, utopia is achieved through love that links personal sensibility to an ideal dimension. Acutely sensing the bleakness of modern existence, both writers project their desire for utopian possibility through the mediation of love. This utopia is fully charged with a desire for freedom, which is at the core of cosmopolitanism. Besides the fact that cosmopolitanism is utopian, both ideas of utopia and cosmopolitanism are driven by a sociopolitical responsibility to engage with the world.

Cosmopolitanism always involves the transformation of existing local orders. Love in Lawrence and Chang also includes this transformative impulse but more importantly contains a healing and generative force. Their writings suggest an alternative mode of cosmopolitanism in which love erodes and dissolves the preexisting human relations to establish new ones, thereby intervening into sociopolitical orders locally and globally.

The discourse of cosmopolitanism is dominated by the idea that the world can come together through the establishment of a universal culture that would be free of the prejudices and particularities of local cultures. Such a project seems to require all peoples to set aside their loves in order to perceive a greater good that is free of subjective desires. This denial of love not only is simply unrealistic but also undermines the very impulses that move people toward the good. At the same time, a blanket affirmation of free love oversimplifies love as a universal feeling and naively believes that world peace can be achieved if everyone simply loves each other.

By contrast, Lawrence and Chang follow the traceable traditions regarding the idea of love in their respective cultures and thereby position love as the key to engage with the world in a way that can transcend boundaries yet also achieve specific visions of freedom. Rather than considering cosmopolitanism as a way to escape from personal bonds, Lawrence and Chang reveal a path that considers love as the basis for new types of relationships that can be mapped out by the utopian imagination. On the one hand, utopia creates a link between private concerns and public problems in which the desire for love is the driver of visions of utopia. On the other hand, utopia creates a relationship between present situation and either imagined future or remembered past. This temporal relationship is one that allows for emancipation from the present reality. Both spatial expansion and a temporal emancipation from the present are driven by a longing for utopia that is grounded in love.

Just as utopia does not appear directly in Lawrence's or Chang's work but only the longing for utopia, the point of cosmopolitan love is not the realization of cosmopolitanism but the maintenance of the longing. Utopia in Lawrence does not appear as a permanent state but happens in a short moment and then quickly disappears. Yet, there is always the constant yearning for utopia again in a contingent future. Lawrence's yearning for utopia is often misunderstood as a declaration of the absolute actualization of utopia, leading to harsh criticism by those who believe him to be a fascist, with Bertrand Russell famously declaring that Lawrence "led straight to Auschwitz."[8] Chang's quiet longing for ideal love creates the connection between a situation of desolation and a vision of utopia. The utopian moment of love for her is also momentary and fleeting. Through the longing, she and her heroines live on these rare moments of love to survive the darkness of the rest of their lives. Neither of these writers wants to pin down any fixed notion of utopia, nor do they seek a substantialized idea of cosmopolitanism. While utopia itself would be a fixed state, the longing for utopia defines a particular relationship that leaves abundant space for possibilities. This mode of cosmopolitan love does not try to offer a solution but rather an attitude that welcomes a plasticity of the utopian vision.

Notes

Introduction

1. D. H. Lawrence, *The Letters of D. H. Lawrence, Volume I, September 1901–May 1913*, ed. James T. Boulton (Cambridge: Cambridge University Press, 1979), 546.

2. Eileen Chang (Ailing Zhang 張愛玲), *Written on Water*, ed. Nicole Huang, trans. Andrew F. Jones (New York: Columbia University Press, 2005), 18. The original Chinese is excerpted from Eileen Chang, *Zhang Ailing diancang quanji* 張愛玲典藏全集 (*The Complete Works of Zhang Ailing*) (Taipei: Huangguan, 2001), 8:91. Hereafter abbreviated as *Quanji*.

3. Plato, *The Symposium: A New Translation by W. Hamilton*, trans. Walter Hamilton (Harmondsworth: Penguin, 1951), 86.

4. C. S. Lewis, *The Allegory of Love: A Study in Medieval Tradition* (Oxford: Clarendon, 1936), 5, 71, 94. See also C. S. Lewis, *The Four Loves* (London: Geoffrey Bles, 1960), 18.

5. Denis de Rougemont, *Love in the Western World* (New York: Pantheon, 1956), 42.

6. Niklas Luhmann, *Love as Passion: The Codification of Intimacy*, trans. Jeremy Gaines (Cambridge, MA: Harvard University Press, 1987). See also Catherine Belsey, *Desire: Love Stories in Western Culture* (Oxford: Blackwell, 1994), and David R. Shumway, *Modern Love: Romance, Intimacy, and the Marriage Crisis* (New York: New York University Press, 2003).

7. See Irving Singer, *The Nature of Love* (Chicago: University of Chicago Press, 1984).

8. In *On Narcissism*, Freud observes that when the sexual instinct is inhibited, overvaluation "spreads over into the psychological sphere: the subject becomes, as it were, intellectually infatuated (that is, his powers of judgment are weakened) by the mental achievements and perfections of the sexual object and he submits to the latter's judgments with credulity." Sigmund Freud, *On Narcissism: An Introduction*, in *The Standard Edition of the Complete Psychological Works of Sigmund Freud*, ed. James Strachey (London: Hogarth, 1953–74), 14:67–104, here 94.

9. I here use the title of Haiyan Lee's book *Revolution of the Heart: A Genealogy of Love in China, 1900–1950* (Stanford: Stanford University Press, 2007). Before 1900, where Lee's study starts, China had undergone a major revolution of the heart, that is, the cult of *qing*.

10. For more details about the cult of *qing*, see Halvor Eifring, *Love and Emotions in Traditional Chinese Literature* (Leiden: Brill, 2003), and Maram Epstein, *Competing Discourses: Orthodoxy, Authenticity, and Engendered Meanings in Late Imperial Chinese Fiction* (Cambridge, MA: Harvard University Asia Center, Harvard University Press, 2001).

11. Denis de Rougemont asserts: "Love, such as we understand it since our twelfth century, does not even have a name in their language. In Chinese the nearest approach to our verb 'to love' is a word which denotes the relationship between a mother and her son. . . . From the viewpoint of the idea of love, there are really two worlds, the Oriental and the Occidental." Denis de Rougemont, "Love," in *Dictionary of the History of Ideas*, ed. Philip Wiener (New York: Scribner, 1973), 3:100. Irving Singer also claims: "In ancient Eastern philosophy . . . the *eros* tradition scarcely existed. Correspondingly, the East did not develop the concept of love in ways that are comparable to those of the West." Singer, *The Nature of Love*, 1:150–51.

12. Her great-grandfather was Li Hongzhang 李鴻章, an influential official in the Qing dynasty. However, her parents' divorce, her father's addiction to opium, and the domestic violence she underwent rendered Chang's family dysfunctional and stifling. See Chang, *Written on Water*.

13. Lawrence, *Letters of D. H. Lawrence, Volume I*, 492.

14. Chang, *Written on Water*, 18.

15. Laurence Lerner, "Lawrence and the Feminists," *D. H. Lawrence: Centenary Essays*, ed. Mara Kalnins (Bristol: Bristol Classical, 1986), 69.

16. Frank Kermode, *Lawrence* (London: Fontana/Collins, 1973), 136.

17. Kate Millett denounces Lawrence as "the most talented and fervid of sexual politicians." Kate Millett, *Sexual Politics* (Garden City, NY: Doubleday, 1970), 239. She believes that sexual dominion is the most prevalent ideology that holds power in culture and associates sexuality (sexual awareness) with radical social change. Though acknowledging Lawrence's lifelong hostility to industrialism and his utopian search for radical political revolution, Millett interprets Lawrence as a complex opponent of feminism whose consciousness was shaped by unconscious personal difficulties and a consciously defensive relation to feminism.

18. Simone de Beauvoir, "D. H. Lawrence or Phallic Pride," in *The Second Sex*, trans. H. M. Parshley (New York: Knopf, 1957), 214.

19. Hilary Simpson, *D. H. Lawrence and Feminism* (DeKalb: Northern Illinois University Press, 1982).

20. Lerner, "Lawrence and the Feminists," 69.

21. F. R. Leavis, *D. H. Lawrence: Novelist* (New York: Simon & Schuster, 1969), 15.

22. Michael Black, *D. H. Lawrence: The Early Fiction: A Commentary* (Basingstoke: Macmillan, 1986); *D. H. Lawrence: The Early Philosophical Works* (London: Macmillan, 1991); *D. H. Lawrence, Sons and Lovers* (Cambridge: Cambridge University Press, 1992); *Lawrence's England: The Major Fiction, 1913–20* (Basingstoke: Palgrave in association with St. Antony's, Oxford, 2001).

23. Mark Spilka, *The Love Ethic of D. H. Lawrence* (Bloomington: Indiana University Press, 1966), 3.

24. Linda Ruth Williams, *D. H. Lawrence* (Plymouth: Northcote House in Association with the British Council, 1997), 11.

25. Terry Eagleton considers Lawrence hostile to democracy and egalitarianism but never in support of fascism. See Terry Eagleton, *The English Novel: An Introduction* (Malden, MA: Blackwell, 2005), 258–60. A number of intellectuals, Paul Poplawski, Keith Sagar, Charles L. Ross, and Michael Squires, to name a few, contribute substantial scholarship to facilitate readers' understanding and academic research about Lawrence.

26. Julia Lovell, "Editor's Afterword," in *Lust, Caution and Other Stories* by Eileen Chang, ed. Julia Lovell (London: Penguin, 2007), 157.

27. Mao Zedong posited that political criteria should be privileged over artistic criteria. Bonnie S. McDougall, *Mao Zedong's "Talks at the Yan'an Conference on Literature and Art": A Translation of the 1943 Text with Commentary* (Ann Arbor: University of Michigan Center for Chinese Studies, 1980).

28. David Der-wei Wang 王德威 has studied Chang's literary works since the 1980s. He initiated the research on the Gothic nature of Chang's fictions. Wang has written numerous forewords for Chang's English literary works—*The Rice Sprout Song, The Rouge of the North, The Sing-song Girls of Shanghai, The Fall of the Pagoda*, and *The Book of Change*. In his foreword for both *The Fall of the Pagoda* and *The Book of Change*, Wang perceives that Chang's most convoluted modernity is hidden in her two semiautobiographical works. Wang grasps Chang's poetics—derivation rather than revelation and involution instead of revolution. Following her Chinese precursors—Han Bangqing and Cao Xueqin—Chang translates her memory of the past into her fictional works. Wang sheds light on Chang's altered ego rather than focusing on authenticity, as previous scholars and readers have. *The Fall of the Pagoda* and *The Book of Change* are derived from Chang's family history but revisited and reinterpreted by Chang several times. As for involution, Chang never ceased her explorations into humanity while remaining skeptical about the revolutionary ideal.

29. Ling Ke 柯灵, "Yaoji Zhang Ailing" 遥寄张爱玲 ("A Letter to Eileen Chang Who Is Far Away"), in *Zhang Ailing quanji* 张爱玲全集 (*Complete Works of Eileen Chang*), ed. Hongda Jin and Qing Yu (Hefei: Anhui wenyi chubanshe, 1996), 947–52.

30. Wenbiao Tang 唐文標, *Zhang Ailing ziliao daquanji* 張愛玲資料大全集 (*The Complete Collection of Materials of Eileen Chang*) (Taipei: Shibao wenhua chuban shiye youxian gongsi, 1984).

31. Zishan Chen 陈子善, *Chenxiang tanxie* 沉香谭屑：张爱玲生平与创作考释 (*Eileen Chang's Life and Works*) (Shanghai: Shanghai shudian chubanshe, 2012); Zishan Chen 陈子善, ed., *Zhang Ailing de fengqi* 张爱玲的风气：1949 年前张爱玲评说 (*The Characteristics of Eileen Chang*) (Ji'nan: Shandong huabao chubanshe, 2004).

32. To name just a few, Jing Shui 水晶, *Zhang Ailing de xiaoshuo yishu* 張愛玲的小說藝術 (*The Art of Eileen Chang's Fiction*) (Taipei: Dadi, 1973); Xingqian Lin 林幸謙, ed., *Zhang Ailing: Wenxue, dianying, wutai* 張愛玲：文學·電影·舞台 (*Eileen Chang: Literature, Film, and the Stage*) (Hong Kong: Oxford University Press, 2007); Shuang Shen, ed., *Lingdu kan Zhang* 零度看張 (*Eileen Chang Degree Zero*) (Hong Kong: Chinese University Press, 2012); Xiaohong Zhang 張小虹, *Wenben Zhang Ailing* 文本張愛玲 (*Textualizing Eileen Chang*) (Taipei: Shibao wenhua chuban qiye gufen youxian gongsi, 2020).

33. C. T. [Chih-tsing] Hsia, *A History of Modern Chinese Fiction, 1917–1957* (New Haven: Yale University Press, 1961), 389.

34. See, for example, Sung-sheng Yvonne Chang, "Yuan Qiongqiong and the Rage

for Eileen Zhang Among Taiwan's 'Feminine' Writers," *Modern Chinese Literature* 4, nos. 1–2 (Spring–Fall 1988): 201–23.

35. "Sealed Off" is included in Martin Puchner, ed., *Norton Anthology of World Literature* (New York: W.W. Norton, 2012), 1345–54.

36. *Stale Mates* is included in David Damrosch, ed., *The Longman Anthology of World Literature* (New York: Longman, 2004), 745–50.

37. Chang was constantly at odds with her time in China as well as in the United States. See Sijia Yao, "The Politics of Literary Fame: Tracing Eileen Chang's Reception in China and the United States," *Forum for World Literature Studies* 8, no. 2 (2016): 291–307.

38. Haiyan Lee, *Revolution of the Heart: A Genealogy of Love in China, 1900–1950* (Stanford: Stanford University Press, 2007), 8. Lee, with the genealogical approach, situates literary expressions of love in social, political, and cultural debates in China in the first half of the twentieth century. Lee borrows Raymond Williams's theory to identify three major "structures of feeling": the Confucian, the enlightenment, and the revolutionary structures (10). The Confucian structure of feeling can be traced back to the cult of *qing* in late Ming, which was inherited by the Mandarin Ducks and Butterfly fiction of the early Republican period. The emotion of love delivers a new sense of humanity but is always confined within a certain ethical Confucian orthodoxy. In the enlightenment structure of feeling, free love is uplifted as a modern idea by the May Fourth movement with the purpose of attacking and dethroning the traditional. In the revolutionary structure of feeling of the 1930s and 1940s romantic love is quickly absorbed into a larger social, political cause.

39. Lawrence, *Letters of D. H. Lawrence, Volume I*, 546.

40. Keith Cushman and Dennis Jackson, "Introduction," in *D. H. Lawrence's Literary Inheritors*, ed. Cushman and Jackson (New York: St. Martin's, 1991), 3.

41. Eileen Chang (Ailing Zhang 張愛玲), *Written on Water*, ed. Nicole Huang, trans. Andrew F. Jones (New York: Columbia University Press, 2005) 18. 我甚至只是寫些男女間的小事情，我的作品裏沒有戰爭，也沒有革命。我以為人在戀愛的時候，是比在戰爭或革命的時候更素樸，也更放恣的。*Quanji*, 8:91.

42. Chang's exposure of disillusions and her rejection of revolution do not mean that she is antiromantic. Edward M. Gunn claims that Chang is antiromantic because "idealized conceptions" such as "heroic characters, revolution, or love" do not appear in Chang's works. Yet, Chang's bleak realities actually foreground the idealized idea of utopia and love, which is another kind of romanticism that differs from the May Fourth revolutionary romanticism. Edward Gunn, *Unwelcome Muse: Chinese Literature in Shanghai and Peking (1937–1945)* (New York: Columbia University Press, 1980), 198.

43. Harold Bloom, "Introduction," in *D. H. Lawrence's "Women in Love,"* ed. Bloom (New York: Chelsea House, 1988), 7.

44. D. H. Lawrence, *Apocalypse and the Writings on Revelation*, ed. Mara Kalnins (London: Cambridge University Press, 1980), 149.

45. Chang, *Written on Water*, 199.

46. Chang, *Quanji*, 8:30.

47. Mike Featherstone, "Love and Eroticism: An Introduction," in *Love and Eroticism*, ed. Featherstone (London: Sage, 1999), 1–19.

48. Immanuel Kant, *Toward Perpetual Peace and Other Writings on Politics, Peace, and History*, ed. Pauline Kleingeld, trans. David L. Colclasure (New Haven: Yale University Press, 2006).

49. David Held, "Principles of Cosmopolitan Order," in *The Cosmopolitanism Reader*, ed. Garrett Wallace Brown and David Held (Cambridge: Polity, 2010), 229–47, here 240–44.

50. Ulrich Beck, *Cosmopolitan Vision*, trans. Ciaran Cronin (Cambridge: Polity, 2006), 1–71.

51. Martha C. Nussbaum, "Kant and Cosmopolitanism," in *Perpetual Peace: Essays on Kant's Cosmopolitan Ideal*, ed. James Bohmann and Matthias Lutz-Bachmann (Cambridge, MA: MIT Press, 1997), 25–57, here 44.

52. Nussbaum, "Kant and Cosmopolitanism," 45.

53. Martha C. Nussbaum, *For Love of Country*, ed. Joshua Cohen (Boston: Beacon, 1996), 15. In a similar move of dissolving love into a love for humanity, Erich Fromm denies the conventional acknowledgment of love as an emotion. Rather, he claims love as the capacity for "care, responsibility, respect, and knowledge." Erich Fromm, *The Art of Loving* (New York: Harper & Row, 1956), 24.

54. Sara Ahmed pursues a similar approach to love by seeing it as a fixation on likeness that promotes nationalism as a racist phenomenon. Sara Ahmed, *The Cultural Politics of Emotion*, 2nd ed. (New York: Routledge, 2015), 122–29.

55. Nussbaum revises her views later on in order to accept the importance of nationalism for pursuing cosmopolitan goals due to the symbolic importance of appeals to patriotism, as long as we "ask ourselves how far we are entitled to devote ourselves to the particular people and places whom we love." She accepts here the legitimacy of love, though she still hesitates to grant such love an intrinsic value. Martha C. Nussbaum, "Toward a Globally Sensitive Patriotism," *Daedalus* 137, no. 3 (Summer 2008): 78–93, here 80.

56. David Miller, *National Responsibility and Global Justice* (Oxford: Oxford University Press, 2007), 43–44.

57. Kwame Anthony Appiah, *Cosmopolitanism: Ethics in a World of Strangers* (New York: W. W. Norton, 2006), 11, 57–67.

58. Appiah, *Cosmopolitanism*, 163.

59. Appiah, *Cosmopolitanism*, 70–72.

60. Appiah, *Cosmopolitanism*, 98.

61. Appiah, *Cosmopolitanism*, 99.

62. Appiah, *Cosmopolitanism*, 153.

63. Appiah, *Cosmopolitanism*, 87–90, 148–51.

64. See, for example, David Porter, *Ideographia: The Chinese Cipher in Early Modern Europe* (Stanford: Stanford University Press, 2001), and Haun Saussy, *Great Walls of Discourse and Other Adventures in Cultural China* (Cambridge, MA: Harvard University Press, 2001).

65. Saussy, *Great Walls of Discourse*, 2.

66. Saussy, *Great Walls of Discourse*, 3.

67. Cf. Shu-mei Shih, "World Studies and Relational Comparison," *PMLA* 130, no. 2 (2015): 430–38, here 437.

68. *Hanyu da cidian* 漢語大詞典, vol. 5, pt. 1, ed. Zhufeng Luo (Shanghai: Hanyu da cidian chubanshe, 2001), 259.《周礼·天官·内宰》:"比其大小與其麤良，而賞罰之。" The English translation is mine.

69. While she does not propose the idea of a third term as a basis for comparison, Chunjie Zhang develops a related mode of comparison in her description of a compositional attempt to find commonalities between China and the West. See Chunjie Zhang, "Introduction: Latour's Compositionism and Global Modernism," in *Composing Modernist Connections in China and Europe*, ed. Zhang (New York: Routledge, 2019), 1–11, here 4.

70. Lawrence studies in China have also been developing since the 1930s. China's first International D. H. Lawrence Conference was held in Shanghai in 1988, where the D. H. Lawrence Society of China was established. Lawrence's works have been translated into Chinese since the 1980s after the ten-year Cultural Revolution in mainland China. For instance, there are over ten Chinese translations of *Women in Love*. See Xianzhi Liu's "Lawrence in China," which also compares Lawrence's *Lady Chatterley's Lover* and Zhang Xianliang's *A Man's Half Is Woman* (1985). Xianzhi Liu, "Lawrence in China: The Reception of D. H. Lawrence in China," *D. H. Lawrence Review* 23, no. 1 (1991): 37–55, here 37–42. Ming Dong Gu also traces China's reception of Lawrence, particularly in the 1980s, when Chinese intellectuals drew inspiration and courage from Lawrence's works to promote social reform. Ming Dong Gu, "D. H. Lawrence and the Chinese Reader," *D. H. Lawrence Review* 23, no. 1 (1991): 43–47.

71. Lauren Berlant, *Cruel Optimism* (Durham: Duke University Press, 2011), 4. In a similar vein, Kathleen Stewart seeks to provide examples of the kinds of moments that Berlant imagines: "*Something* throws itself together in a moment as an event and a sensation; a something both animated and inhabitable." Kathleen Stewart, *Ordinary Affects* (Durham: Duke University Press, 2007), 1.

72. Berlant, *Cruel Optimism*, 4.

73. Leo Ou-fan Lee, *Cangliang yu shigu: Zhang Ailing de qishi* 蒼涼與世故：張愛玲的啟示 (*Desolation and Sophistication*) (Hong Kong: Oxford University Press, 2006), 79.

Chapter 1

1. Claude Levi-Strauss, *The Elementary Structures of Kinship*, ed. Rodney Needham, trans. James Harle Bell, John Richard von Sturmer, and Rodney Needham (Boston: Beacon, 1969), 47–48.

2. Levi-Strauss argues that the incest prohibition is the link between nature and culture. Levi-Strauss, *Elementary Structures*, 63–64.

3. Although Lacan proposes the opposition between incestuous desire and its prohibition, he still lives in the shadow of the Freudian narrative of the Oedipus complex when he equates prohibition with culture and incestuous desire with nature. See Jacques Lacan, *Écrits: The First Complete Edition in English*, trans. Bruce Fink (New York: Norton, 2006), 228–30.

4. Jacques Derrida, *Of Grammatology*, trans. Gayatri Chakravorty Spivak (Baltimore: Johns Hopkins University Press, 1974), 267.

5. Andrew Plaks, "The Problem of Incest in *Jin Ping Mei* and *Honglou meng*," in *Paradoxes of Traditional Chinese Literature*, ed. Eva Hung (Hong Kong: Chinese University Press, 1994), 126.

6. Plaks, "Problem of Incest," 123–45. In modern China, Cao Yu's play *Leiyu* 雷雨 (*The Thunderstorm*) demonstrates Chinese intellectuals' immense interest in psychoanalysis, even though it has been constantly interpreted as an antitraditional master narrative in the May Fourth era. It vividly reveals human nature and eventually delivers a powerful tragic emotion. "The Heart Sutra," as a precursor text that addresses father-daughter incestuous desire, increases the visibility of actual incestuous desire in public and inspired subsequent Chinese authors to explore the representation of incest. Tong King Lee, in a recent essay, points to three stories by contemporary Chinese women writers, Ouyang Tzu, Wong Bik-wan, and Chen Xue. See Tong King Lee, "Forbidden Imaginations: Three Chinese Narratives on Mother-Son Incest," *Chinese Literature Essays, Articles, Reviews (CLEAR)* 36, no. 4 (2014): 1–24.

7. Xianzhi Liu, "Lawrence in China: The Reception of D. H. Lawrence in China," *D. H. Lawrence Review* 23, no. 1 (1991): 37–55, here 37.

8. "她讲给我听萧伯纳、赫克斯莱、桑茂忒芒，及劳伦斯的作品 [. . . . .]可是他们的好处到底有限制。" My translation. See Lancheng Hu, *Jinsheng jinshi* 今生今世 (*This Life, These Times*) (Beijing: Zhongguo shehui kexue chubanshe, 2003), 157.

9. Sigmund Freud, "A Special Type of Choice of Object Made by Men," in *The Standard Edition of the Complete Psychological Works of Sigmund Freud*, ed. James Strachey (London: Hogarth, 1953–74), 11:163–76, here 171.

10. Sigmund Freud, "On the Universal Tendency to Debasement in the Sphere of Love," in *The Standard Edition*, ed. Strachey, 11:177–90.

11. D. H. Lawrence, *Sons and Lovers*, ed. Helen Baron and Carl Baron (Cambridge: Cambridge University Press, 1992), 255. Subsequent references to this work are included in the text in parentheses.

12. Eileen Chang, "The Heart Sutra," in "The Parent-Child Relationship in Three Stories by Eileen Chang with a Translation of 'The Heart Sutra,'" by Roslyn Tom (master's thesis, Harvard University, 1985), 70. 她牽著他的袖子，試著把手伸進袖口裏去，幽幽的道：「我是一生一世不打算離開你的。」*Quanji*, 5:265.

13. Chang, "The Heart Sutra," 64. 峯儀道：「我知道你為什麼願意永遠不長大。」[. . . . .] 峯儀低聲道：「你怕你長大了，我們就要生疏了，是不是？」*Quanji*, 5:260.

14. Sigmund Freud, *Three Essays on the Theory of Sexuality*, in *Standard Edition*, ed. Strachey, 225.

15. Chang, "The Heart Sutra," 91. 她的腿緊緊壓在她母親的腿上——自己的骨肉！她突然感到一陣強烈的厭惡與恐怖。怕誰？恨誰？她母親？她自己？她們只是愛著同一個男子的兩個女人。她憎嫌她自己的肌肉與那緊緊擠著她的、溫暖的、他人的肌肉。呵，她自己的母親！*Quanji*, 5:281–82.

16. Mark Spilka, "Counterfeit Loves," in *Twentieth Century Interpretations of Sons and Lovers: A Collection of Critical Essays*, ed. Judith Farr (Englewood Cliffs, NJ: Prentice-Hall, 1970), 51–63.

17. Daniel A. Weiss, "The Mother in the Mind," in *Twentieth Century Interpretations*, ed. Farr, 28–41. Frederick Hoffman, "Lawrence's Quarrel with Freud," in *The Achievement of D. H. Lawrence*, ed. Frederick Hoffman and Harry T. Moore (Norman: University of Oklahoma Press, 1953), 106–27. Shirley Panken, "Some Psychodynamics in *Sons*

and Lovers: A New Look at the Oedipal Theme," *Psychoanalytic Review* 61, no. 4 (1974): 571–89.

18. Alfred Booth Kuttner, "Sons and Lovers: A Freudian Appreciation," *Psychoanalytic Review* 3 (July 1916): 295–317.

19. Geoffrey Harvey, *Sons and Lovers (Critics Debate)* (Atlantic Highlands, NJ: Humanities Press, 1987), 9.

20. Gāmini Salgādo, *D. H. Lawrence: Sons and Lovers* (London: Macmillan, 1969), 25.

21. Lawrence gained secondhand knowledge of Freud's theory from his wife, Frieda, along with some psychoanalytical scholars, such as Otto Gross, Barbara Low, David Eder, and Ernest Jones. Frederick Hoffman in *Freudianism and the Literary Mind* reveals that when Lawrence prepared for his final draft of *Sons and Lovers*, Frieda and Lawrence had a long discussion about Freud, which led Lawrence to position the mother-son relationship at the center and finally change the title. As Andrew Harrison also observes, Lawrence's "traveling with her [Frieda] to Germany and her second-hand knowledge of Freudian psychoanalysis both enabled him to see his novel differently: not only as transformed autobiography, but as a depiction of male sexuality and psychological disturbance comparable to Oedipus Tyrannus or Hamlet." Andrew Harrison, *D. H. Lawrence: "Sons and Lovers." Literature Insights* (Tirril: Humanities-Ebooks, 2007), 10.

22. Wendy Larson, *From Ah Q to Lei Feng: Freud and Revolutionary Spirit in 20th Century China* (Stanford: Stanford University Press, 2009), 32.

23. Larson, *From Ah Q to Lei Feng*, 72–73.

24. Larson, *From Ah Q to Lei Feng*, 72. See also Jingyuan Zhang, *Psychoanalysis in China: Literary Transformations 1919–1949* (Ithaca, NY: Cornell East Asia Series, Cornell University, 1992), 126–27.

25. Lawrence's letter to Barbara Low, September 16, 1916. D. H. Lawrence, *The Letters of D. H. Lawrence, Volume II, June 1913–October 1916*, ed. George J. Zytaruk and James T. Boulton (Cambridge: Cambridge University Press, 2002), 655.

26. Frederick Hoffman, *Freudianism and the Literary Mind* (Baton Rouge: Louisiana State University Press, 1957), 153.

27. Spilka, "Counterfeit Loves," 52.

28. D. H. Lawrence, *Psychoanalysis and the Unconscious and Fantasia of the Unconscious*, ed. Bruce Steele (Cambridge: Cambridge University Press, 2004).

29. Anne Fernihough, *D. H. Lawrence: Aesthetics and Ideology* (Oxford: Clarendon, 1993), 67.

30. Lawrence believes that there is a polarity of the upper "sympathetic centres" and the lower "voluntary centres." In "Parent Love," he explains this sympathy-voluntary polarity: "For all the children who matter, a steady and persistent pressure upon the upper sympathetic centres, and a steady and persistent starving of the lower centres, particularly the great voluntary centre of the lower body. The centre of sensual, manly independence, of exultation in the sturdy, defiant self, wilfulness and masterfulness and pride, this centre is steadily suppressed. The warm, swift sensual self is steadily and persistently denied, damped, weakened, throughout all the period of childhood." Lawrence, *Psychoanalysis and the Unconscious*, 142.

31. Lawrence, *Psychoanalysis and the Unconscious*, 147–48.

32. Lawrence, *Psychoanalysis and the Unconscious*, 142.

33. Lawrence, *Psychoanalysis and the Unconscious*, 142.

34. Lawrence, *Psychoanalysis and the Unconscious*, 144.

35. Lawrence, *Psychoanalysis and the Unconscious*, 13–14.

36. Lawrence, *Psychoanalysis and the Unconscious*, 151.

37. Lawrence, *Psychoanalysis and the Unconscious*, 148–49.

38. Franco Moretti, "Conjectures on World Literature," *New Left Review* 1 (2000): 54–68, here 66.

39. Eileen Chang, "Demons and Fairies," *XX Century* 5, no. 6 (1943): 421–29, here 423. 對於父母遺體過度的關切，唯一的解釋是：在中國，為人子的感情有著反常的發展。中國人傳統上虛擬的孝心是一種偉大的、吞沒一切的熱情；既然它是惟一一合法的熱情，它的畸形發達是與他方面的沖淡平靜完全失去了比例的。*Quanji*, 8:51.

40. Chang, "Demons and Fairies," 423. 模範兒子以食人者熱烈的犧牲方式，割股煨湯餵給生病的父母吃。這一類的行為，普通只有瘋狂地戀愛著的人才做得出。*Quanji*, 8:51.

41. 忠 (*zhong*, loyalty), 孝 (*xiao*, filial piety), 節 (*jie*, chastity), and 義 (*yi*, righteousness) are the four virtues Chinese gentlemen tried to cultivate and maintain.

42. Ming Dong Gu, "The Filial Piety Complex: The Oedipus Complex in Chinese Cultural Context," in *The Reception and Rendition of Freud in China: China's Freudian Slip*, ed. Tao Jiang and Philip J. Ivanhoe (New York: Routledge, 2013), 81.

43. Chang, "The Heart Sutra," 63. *Quanji*, 5:259.

44. Paola Zamperini, "A Family Romance: Specters of Incest in Eileen Chang's 'Xinjing,'" *Prism: Theory and Modern Chinese Literature* 17, no. 1 (March 2020): 29.

45. Chang, "The Heart Sutra," 57. 綾卿笑道：「你難道打算做一輩子小孩子?」小寒把下頦一昂道：「我就守在家裡做一輩子孩子，又怎麼著?不見得我家裏有誰容不得我! *Quanji*, 5:254.

46. Chang, "The Heart Sutra," 64. 輕輕用一隻食指沿著他鼻子滑上滑下。*Quanji*, 5:259.

47. Chang, "The Heart Sutra," 73. 「事情是怎樣開頭的，我並不知道。七八年了——你才那麼一點高的時候⋯⋯不知不覺的⋯⋯」啊，七八年前⋯⋯那是最可留戀的時候，父母之愛的黃金時期，沒有猜忌，沒有試探，沒有嫌疑。*Quanji*, 5:267.

48. Chang, "The Heart Sutra," 72. *Quanji*, 5:266.

49. In citing Freud, Lacan, Levi-Strauss, and Derrida to argue that incestuous desire rather than the incest taboo lies at the ground of cultural reproduction, Zamperini focuses attention on Xiaohan's incestuous desire. Zamperini, "Family Romance," 7, 20–21. In doing so, she seems to partially excuse the father as "apparently ignorant and unaware" (7), but in fact the central problem is the failure of the father to enforce the incest prohibition and suppress his own incestuous desires. This Freudian perspective shifts the blame for incest from the father to the daughter.

50. Eileen Chang, "The Golden Cangue," in *Twentieth-Century Chinese Stories*, ed. Chih-tsing Hsia (New York: Columbia University Press, 1971), 174. 這些年來她的生命裏只有這一個男人。只有他，她不怕他想她的錢——橫豎錢都是他的。可是，因為他是她的兒子，他這一個人還抵不了半個⋯⋯現在，就連這半個人她也保留不住——他娶了親。*Quanji*, 5:37.

51. Zamperini, "Family Romance," 15.

Chapter 2

1. F. R. Leavis, *D. H. Lawrence: Novelist* (New York: Simon & Schuster, 1969), 288.

2. According to Cai Dengshan's *Lust, Caution and Eileen*, Chang began writing the story in 1953 but did not publish it until 1978. See Dengshan Cai 蔡登山, *Lust, Caution and Eileen* 色戒愛玲 (Taipei: INK Publishing, 2007), 20.

3. This story, along with its filmic adaptation, has attracted the attention of many major Chinese studies scholars, including Ou-fan Lee, Xiaojue Wang, Haiyan Lee, Nicole Huang, Peng Hsiao-yen, Chang Hsiao-hung, and Hsiu-Chuang Deppman. There is even a whole book devoted to studies of "Lust, Caution": *From Eileen Chang to Ang Lee: Lust/Caution*, ed. Peng Hsiao-yen and Whitney Crothers Dilley (New York: Routledge, 2014).

4. The story, politically unpopular in the Chinese context, does not feed into the patriotic narrative of twentieth-century China. Nicole Huang finds in her copious research on Republican-era literature that "Lust, Caution" is "Chang's only story dealing with wartime politics." It produces "a loudly discordant tune, one that puzzles her critics and forces them to turn away from this story so as to avoid placing it within the context of the literature of her time." Nicole Huang, *Women, War, Domesticity: Shanghai Literature and Popular Culture of the 1940s* (Leiden: Brill, 2005), 218.

5. "Gypsy" is a problematic term but was historically prevalent. In Lawrence's story, the gypsy is emblemized as an "honorable beast," in Peter Balbert's words. In Balbert's latest interpretation of Lawrence's marriage matrix, the gypsy paradoxically combines profane primitivism and religious transcendence. Peter Balbert, *D.H. Lawrence and the Marriage Matrix: Intertextual Adventures in Conflict, Renewal, and Transcendence* (London: Cambridge Scholars, 2016), 206.

6. Leavis, *D. H. Lawrence: Novelist*, 294.

7. D. H. Lawrence, *The Virgin and the Gipsy and Other Stories*, ed. Michael Herbert, Bethan Jones, and Lindeth Vasey (Cambridge: Cambridge University Press, 2005), 16, 6. Subsequent references to this text are included in parentheses after the quote.

8. Nancy Paxton, "Reimagining Melodrama: *The Virgin and the Gipsy* and the Consequences of Mourning," *D. H. Lawrence Review* 38, no. 2 (2013): 58–76, here 60.

9. John Turner, "Purity and Danger in D. H. Lawrence's *The Virgin and the Gipsy*," in *D. H. Lawrence: Centenary Essays*, ed. Mara Kalnins (Bristol: Bristol Classical, 1986), 156.

10. Eileen Chang, *Lust, Caution and Other Stories*, trans. Julia Lovell (London: Penguin, 2007), 28.「到女人心裏的路通過陰道。」*Quanji*, 3:245.

11. Chang, *Lust, Caution*, 28. 那，難道她有點愛上了老易？她不信，但是也無法斬釘截鐵的說不是。*Quanji*, 3:246.

12. Haiyan Lee uses Emmanuel Levinas's notion of "face of the other" to justify Jiazhi's eventual betrayal and transcendence. See Haiyan Lee, "Enemy under My Skin: Eileen Chang's *Lust, Caution* and the Politics of Transcendence," *PMLA* 125, no. 3 (2010): 640–56.

13. Chang, *Lust, Caution*, 30. 這個人是真愛我的，她突然想，心下轟然一聲，若有所失。太晚了[. . . . .]「快走，」她低聲說。*Quanji*, 3:247.

14. Huang, *Women, War, Domesticity*, 218.

15. Chang, *Lust, Caution*, 35. 得一知己，死而無憾。他覺得她的影子會永遠依傍他，安慰他 [. . . . . .] 他們是原始的獵人與獵物的關係，虎與倀的關係，最終極的佔有。她這才生是他的人，死是他的鬼。*Quanji*, 3:251.

16. The Motion Picture Association of America rated this film as NC-17, categorized as adults only, because it contains several highly explicit sensual scenes.

17. Ang Lee, "Afterword," *Lust, Caution: The Story* by Eileen Chang (New York: Anchor, 2007), 59.

18. Hsiu-Chuang Deppman, "Seduction of a Filmic Romance," in *Eileen Chang: Romancing Languages, Cultures and Genres*, ed. Kam Louie (Hong Kong: Hong Kong University Press, 2012), 155–76, here 155.

19. Irving Singer, *The Nature of Love* (Chicago: University of Chicago Press, 1984), 3:228. The modern philosopher Irving Singer devotes three volumes to exploring the nature of Western love in different times, from Greek love (*éros, philía*, and *agápe*), Christian love, courtly love, and romantic love to modern love.

20. Kingsley Widmer, *Defiant Desire: Some Dialectical Legacies of D. H. Lawrence* (Carbondale: Southern Illinois University Press, 1992), 8.

21. Perry Link also senses Chang's awareness of the political system, especially the way that the system affects private thoughts. Link observes that Chang seems "like George Orwell, to have almost a sixth sense for immediate comprehension of what an authoritarian political system will do to human beings in daily life. She looks past the grand political system itself and focuses instead on the lives of people—how they feel and behave as they adapt to what the system forces upon them." Perry Link, "Mao's China: The Language Game," *New York Review of Books*, May 15, 2015.

22. James Adams, "Victorian Sexualities," in *A Companion to Victorian Literature & Culture*, ed. Herbert F. Tucker (Malden, MA: Blackwell, 1999), 125–38, here 130.

23. Adams, "Victorian Sexualities," 127.

24. "Now according to Nietzsche (and Hegel before him), the slave's morality is, at its most effective, Christianity." Garry Watson, "'The Fact, and the Crucial Significance, of Desire': Lawrence's 'Virgin and the Gipsy,'" *English* 34 (summer 1985): 131–56, here 136.

25. David Craig, *The Real Foundations: Literature and Social Change* (New York: Oxford University Press, 1974), 29.

26. John Robert Reed, *Victorian Conventions* (Athens: Ohio University Press, 1975), 397.

27. Drew Milne, "Lawrence and the Politics of Sexual Politics," in *The Cambridge Companion to D. H. Lawrence*, ed. Anne Fernihough (Cambridge: Cambridge University Press, 2001), 197–216, here 202.

28. This literary policing conducted by Chinese nationalists resembles the critical blinders worn by masculinist African American intellectuals. Ann duCille in her illuminating book *The Coupling Convention* examines the critical invisibility of the marriage theme, or "sexual reticence," in early African American women writers' novels. Ann duCille, *The Coupling Convention: Sex, Text, and Tradition in Black Women's Fiction* (New York: Oxford University Press, 1993), 10. Chinese women writers in semi-colonized China faced the same double jeopardy (race and gender) as early African American women writers did. As subversive as the "coupling convention" used by early African American women's novels, Chang's stories, with themes of love and marriage, also dramatize defiance against patriarchy as well as masculinist discourse.

29. See Amy Dooling, *Women's Literary Feminism in Twentieth Century China* (New York: Palgrave Macmillan, 2005), 98–102.

30. Leo Ou-fan Lee, *Shanghai Modern: The Flowering of a New Urban Culture in China, 1930–1945* (Cambridge, MA: Harvard University Press, 1999), 269.

31. Julia Lovell, "Editor's Afterword," in *Lust, Caution and Other Stories* by Eileen Chang, ed. Julia Lovell (London: Penguin, 2007), 159.

32. Lovell, "Editor's Afterword," 157.

33. Whitney Crothers Dilley, "The 'Real' Wang Jiazhi: Taboo, Transgression, and Truth in Lust/Caution," in *Eileen Chang to Ang Lee: Lust, Caution*, ed. Xiaoyan Peng and Whitney Crothers Dilley (New York: Routledge, 2014), 121–32, here 130.

34. Chang's case illustrates Fredric Jameson's theory of national allegory. Jameson believes that private individual destiny in fiction embodies an allegory of public third world society. See Fredric Jameson, "Third-World Literature in the Era of Multinational Capitalism," *Social Text* 15, no. 3 (1986): 65–88.

35. Huang, *Women, War, Domesticity*, 16.

36. Haiyan Lee, "Eileen Chang's Poetics of the Social: Review of *Love in a Fallen City*," Modern Chinese Literature and Culture (MCLC) Resource Center, Ohio State University, 2007, http://u.osu.edu/mclc/book-reviews/review-of-love-in-a-fallen-city/

37. Carol Siegel, "Floods of Female Desire in Lawrence and Eudora Welty," in *D. H. Lawrence's Literary Inheritors*, ed. Cushman and Jackson (New York: St. Martin's, 1991), 109–30, here 126.

38. Baruch Hochman, *Another Ego: The Changing View of Self and Society in the Work of D. H. Lawrence* (Columbia: University of South Carolina Press, 1970), 83.

Chapter 3

1. Chinese literary modernity differs significantly from its Western counterpart in the twentieth century. The semicolonized status of China at the turn of the twentieth century compelled Chinese intellectuals to embrace Westernization, especially science, democracy, and industry, the ideologies that Western literary modernity criticized and repudiated. Kirk Denton acknowledges, "The slowness of historical modernity's arrival and the obsession among Chinese with bringing it about in order to restore to China its lost cultural grandeur precluded the emergence of an antagonistic literary modernity. . . . The Western and Chinese literary experiences in the twentieth century are fundamentally different." Kirk Denton, *Modern Chinese Literary Thought: Writings on Literature, 1893–1945* (Stanford: Stanford University Press, 1996), 59. The May Fourth Movement, commonly acknowledged as the apex of Chinese literary modernity, worshipped science and democracy and subordinated literature to political and social agendas. However, Eileen Chang, considered another voice opposed to the dominant May Fourth nationalist ideals, presents another picture of Chinese modernity.

2. I adopt Leo Ou-fan Lee's 李歐梵 translation, "de-cadenced contrast," for 參差的對照. Lee offers the term in his *Cangliang yu shigu* 蒼涼與世故 (*Desolation and Sophistication*) (Hong Kong: Oxford University Press, 2006), 79.

3. D. H. Lawrence, *Lady Chatterley's Lover*, ed. Michael Squires (Cambridge: Cambridge University Press, 1993), 18. Subsequent references to this text will be inserted after the quote in parentheses.

4. D. H. Lawrence, *Reflections on the Death of a Porcupine and Other Essays*, ed. Michael Herbert (Cambridge: Cambridge University Press, 1988), 76, 79.

5. Ian Gregor and Brian Nicholas, *The Moral and the Story* (London: Faber and Faber, 1962), 224.

6. D. H. Lawrence, *Study of Thomas Hardy and Other Essays*, ed. Bruce Steele (Cambridge: Cambridge University Press, 1985), 204.

7. D. H. Lawrence, *Late Essays and Articles*, ed. James T. Boulton (Cambridge: Cambridge University Press, 2004), 282.

8. Keith Cushman describes how the themes of *Lady Chatterley's Lover* developed out of Lawrence's previous work on *The Virgin and the Gipsy*. Keith Cushman, "The Virgin and the Gipsy and the Lady and the Gamekeeper," in *D. H. Lawrence's "Lady": A New Look at Lady Chatterley's Lover*, ed. Michael Squires and Dennis Jackson (Athens: University of Georgia Press 1985), 154–69.

9. "At one time Lawrence was going to give this novel the title Tenderness, and there is a good deal in the text as we have it to suggest why." Colin Clarke, *River of Dissolution: D. H. Lawrence and English Romanticism* (London: Routledge and Kegan Paul, 1969), 143.

10. D. H. Lawrence, *The Letters of D. H. Lawrence, Volume VI, March 1927–November 1928*, ed. James T. Boulton and Margaret Boulton with Gerald M. Lacy (Cambridge: Cambridge University Press, 1991), 321.

11. John B. Humma, "The Interpenetrating Metaphor: Nature and Myth in *Lady Chatterley's Lover*," *PMLA* 98, no. 1 (1983): 77–86, here 77.

12. D. H. Lawrence, "A Propos of 'Lady Chatterley's Lover,'" in *Lady Chatterley's Lover*, ed. Michael Squires (Cambridge: Cambridge University Press, 1993), 323.

13. Lawrence, *Lady Chatterley's Lover*, 323.

14. Clarke, *River of Dissolution*, 138.

15. Kingsley Widmer, *Defiant Desire: Some Dialectical Legacies of D. H. Lawrence* (Carbondale: Southern Illinois University Press, 1992), 70.

16. Eileen Chang (Ailing Zhang 張愛玲), *Written on Water*, ed. Nicole Huang, trans. Andrew F. Jones (New York: Columbia University Press, 2005), 16–17. The original Chinese is excerpted from Chang, *Quanji*, 8:89.

17. Chang, *Quanji*, 8:235–36. My translation.

18. "She can be as gay and satiric as Jane Austen, but behind her comic surface is a profound impersonal sorrow over the perversity and pettiness of all passions. It is this astonishing combination—a Chaucerian gusto for life and all its little enjoyments plus an adult and tragic awareness of the human condition—that marks the young author of *Romances* as a well-nigh unique figure in modern Chinese literature." C. T. Hsia, *A History of Modern Chinese Fiction, 1917–1957* (New Haven: Yale University Press, 1961), 392–93.

19. Eileen Chang, "The Golden Cangue" in *Twentieth-Century Chinese Stories*, ed. C. T. Hsia (New York: Columbia University Press, 1971), 138–91, here 189. Hsia uses Wade-Giles romanization for proper names. However, I am using *pinyin* romanization in this study. *Quanji*, 5:52.

20. Chang, "The Golden Cangue," 150. 「你去挨著你二哥坐坐！你去挨著你二哥坐坐！[......]「你碰過他的肉沒有？是軟的、重的，就像人的腳有時發麻了，摸上去那感覺......」*Quanji*, 5:15.

21. Chang, "The Golden Cangue," 157. *Quanji*, 5:22.

22. Chang, "The Golden Cangue," 150. *Quanji*, 5:16.

23. Chang, "The Golden Cangue," 151. 她睜著眼直勾勾朝前望著，耳朵上的實心小金墜子像兩隻銅釘把她釘在門上——玻璃匣子裏蝴蝶的標本，鮮艷而悽愴。*Quanji*, 5:16.

24. Chang, "The Golden Cangue," 151. *Quanji*, 5:16–17.

25. Change, "The Golden Cangue," 156–57. 「我們這位姑奶奶怎麼換了個人？沒出嫁的時候不過要強些，嘴頭上瑣碎些，就連後來我們去瞧她，雖是比前暴躁些，也還有個分寸，不似如今瘋瘋傻傻，說話有一句沒一句，就沒一點兒得人心的地方。」*Quanji*, 5:21.

26. Chang, "The Golden Cangue," 163. *Quanji*, 5:27–28.

27. Lee, *Shanghai Modern*, 289.

28. Chang, "The Golden Cangue," 166. 酸梅湯沿著桌子一滴一滴朝下滴，像遲遲的夜漏——一滴，一滴......一更，二更......一年，一百年。真長，這寂寂的一剎那。*Quanji*, 5:30.

29. Chang, "The Golden Cangue," 182. *Quanji*, 5:45.

30. Chang, "The Golden Cangue," 188. 直覺地感到那是個瘋子——無緣無故的，他只是毛骨悚然。*Quanji*, 5:51.

31. Chang, "The Golden Cangue," 189. 長安靜靜的跟在他後面送了出來*Quanji*, 5:52.

32. Chang, "The Golden Cangue," 189. 她的藏青長袖旗袍上有著淡黃的雛菊*Quanji*, 5:52.

33. Chang, "The Golden Cangue," 170, 186. 一個美麗的，蒼涼的手勢 *Quanji*, 5:34，一個美麗而蒼涼的手勢 49.

34. Tonglin Lu offers an overview of the literary climate during that time. "Among the problems created by the prevailing masculinism of May Fourth intellectuals was an indifferent if not hostile attitude toward women's new role as writers. For women writers, preoccupation with gender-related problems typically earned them the criticism that they indulged in the insignificance of the private sphere." Tonglin Lu, *Gender and Sexuality in Twentieth-Century Chinese Literature and Society* (Albany: State University of New York Press, 1993), 6. Chang's gynocentric writing style not only mirrors actual heterosexual relations in China but also counteracts the masculinist policing.

35. Wendy Larson, *Women and Writing in Modern China* (Stanford: Stanford University Press, 1998), 195–97, here 197. Larson's feminist, historical, and literary study examines the extent to which the gender hierarchy, characterized as the gendered dichotomy of *de* (moral virtue) and *cai* (literary talent), was maintained, disturbed, or mobilized in Chinese women's writing in early twentieth-century China. Larson interprets Qiqiao as a "testimony to the persistence of moral virtue" (196). If Qiqiao had a way to channel her energies into literary production, then she might have found fulfillment in her life. But because she does not have this possibility, her continuing adherence to an ideal of moral virtue leads her to suppress her desires by developing a defiant violence that expresses itself as a self-destructive tendency.

36. Chang, *Written on Water*, 199. 快，快，遲了來不及了，來不及了！*Quanji*, 8:30.

37. Chang, *Written on Water*, 199. 個人即使等得及，時代是倉卒的，已經在破壞中，還有更大的破壞要來。有一天我們的文明，不論是昇華還是浮華，都要成為過去。如果我最常用的字是「荒涼」，那是因為思想背景裏有這惘惘的威脅。*Quanji*, 8:30.

38. Her exclusive literary interest in love and woman's subjectivity was derided and rejected by mainstream Chinese intellectuals in the 1940s. As Ou-fan Lee observes, Chang's "intellectual background" is "never anticipated by the 'symphonic' conductors of the May Fourth movement." Lee, *Shanghai Modern*, 288. As the school of Mandarin Ducks and Butterflies was restored to glory by Perry Link in the 1980s, Chang's literary practice and aesthetic value have been unearthed and appreciated more and more since the 1990s.

39. Chang, *Written on Water*, 16. *Quanji*, 8:89.

40. Lee, *Shanghai Modern*, 284.

41. Rey Chow, *Woman and Chinese Modernity: The Politics of Reading between West and East* (Minneapolis: University of Minnesota Press, 1991), 84, 85.

42. Chang, "The Golden Cangue," 138. 再好的月色也不免帶點淒涼 *Quanji*, 5:5.

Chapter 4

1. Eileen Chang, *Xiao tuanyuan* 小團圓 (*The Little Reunion*) (Taipei: Huangguan, 2009). *The Little Reunion* was written between 1975 and 1976 but was published in Hong Kong and Mainland China in 2009. English translations for this book are my own.

2. 金色的永生 is a term I borrow from Chang to describe the utopian existence Chang pines for. Change, *Xiao tuanyuan*, 172.

3. Sarah Urang, *Kindled in the Flame: The Apocalyptic Scene in D. H. Lawrence* (Ann Arbor, MI: UMI Research, 1983). P. T. Whelan, *D. H. Lawrence: Myth and Metaphysic in "The Rainbow" and "Women in Love"* (Ann Arbor, MI: UMI Research, 1988). John B. Humma, "Lawrence in Another Light: *Women in Love* and Existentialism," *Studies in the Novel* 24, no. 4 (1992): 392–409.

4. Harold Bloom, *D. H. Lawrence's "Women in Love"* (New York: Chelsea House, 1988), 1.

5. Clara Iwasaki, *Rethinking the Modern Chinese Canon: Refractions across the Transpacific* (Amherst, NY: Cambria Press, 2020), 149–85.

6. Deborah Tze-lan Sang, "Romancing Rhetoricity and Historicity: The Representational Politics and Poetics of *Little Reunion*," in *Eileen Chang: Romancing Languages, Cultures and Genres*, ed. Kam Louie (Hong Kong: Hong Kong University Press, 2012), 193–213, here 213.

7. Jiwei Xiao, "Belated Reunion? Eileen Chang, Late Style and World Literature," *New Left Review*, no. 111 (May-June 2018): 89–110, here 99–101.

8. Plato, *The Symposium: A New Translation by W. Hamilton*, trans. Walter Hamilton (Harmondsworth: Penguin, 1951), 64.

9. D. H. Lawrence, *Women in Love*, ed. David Farmer, Lindeth Vasey, and John Worthen (Cambridge: Cambridge University Press, 1987) 152, cited hereafter with page numbers in parentheses.

10. This reminds us of Nietzsche's illuminating insight into modern human tragedy at the end of *The Birth of Tragedy*: "Man today, stripped of myth, stands famished among all his pasts and must dig frantically for roots, be it among the most remote antiquities." Friedrich Nietzsche, *The Birth of Tragedy and The Genealogy of Morals*, trans. Francis Golffing (New York: Anchor, 1990), 137. Modern people lost their vital tie with history

and nature, and they can only move backward and downward to search for their lost origin—the mythic home or the mythic womb. Lawrence seems to resolve the tragic situation of modern humanity through the deepest connection between man and woman.

11. D. H. Lawrence, "Sleep and Dreams," in *Psychoanalysis and the Unconscious and Fantasia of the Unconscious*, ed. Bruce Steele (Cambridge: Cambridge University Press, 2004), 185.

12. D. H. Lawrence, *Lady Chatterley's Lover*, ed. Michael Squires (Cambridge: Cambridge University Press, 1993), 325.

13. Eleanor Green explores the kinship between Lawrence and Schopenhauer in two essays: "Schopenhauer and D. H. Lawrence on Sex and Love," *D. H. Lawrence Review* 8 (Fall 1975): 329–45, and "Lawrence, Schopenhauer, and the Dual Nature of the Universe," *South Atlantic Bulletin* 62 (Nov. 1977): 84–92. Nietzsche's influence on Lawrence has been discussed in Colin Milton's *Lawrence and Nietzsche: A Study in Influence* (Aberdeen: Aberdeen University Press, 1987), and Kingsley Widmer, *Defiant Desire: Some Dialectical Legacies of D. H. Lawrence* (Carbondale: Southern Illinois University Press, 1992), 40–69.

14. Gerald Doherty attempts to offer a detailed analysis of Lawrence's attitude toward Buddhism from 1908 to 1929. David Pitre approaches *Women in Love* from the perspective of Taoism. See Gerald Doherty, "The Nirvana Dimension: D. H. Lawrence's Quarrel with Buddhism," *D. H. Lawrence Review* 15, nos. 1–2 (1982): 51–76. David Pitre, "The Mystical Lawrence: Rupert Birkin's Taoist Quest," *Studies in Mystical Literature* 3, no. 1 (1983): 43–64.

15. William York Tindall, "Transcendentalism in Contemporary Literature," in *The Asian Legacy and American Life*, ed. Arthur Christy (New York: John Day, 1945), 175–92, here 175.

16. D. H. Lawrence, *Study of Thomas Hardy and Other Essays*, ed. Bruce Steele (Cambridge: Cambridge University Press, 1985), 78.

17. Lawrence, "A Propos of 'Lady Chatterley's Lover,'" *Lady Chatterley's Lover*, 325.

18. D. H. Lawrence, *The Letters of D. H. Lawrence, Volume I, September 1901–May 1913*, ed. James T. Boulton (Cambridge: Cambridge University Press, 1979), 492.

19. Hilary Simpson, *D. H. Lawrence and Feminism* (DeKalb: Northern Illinois University Press, 1982), 133. Ed Jewinski also systematically and closely studied the shared view on phallus in the work of Lacan and Lawrence. Ed Jewinski, "The Phallus in D. H. Lawrence and Jacques Lacan," *D. H. Lawrence Review* 21, no. 1 (1989): 7–24. Earl G. Ingersoll devoted a whole book to approaching Lawrence's narrative of desire with Lacan's psychological theory. Earl G. Ingersoll, *D. H. Lawrence, Desire, and Narrative* (Gainesville: University Press of Florida, 2001).

20. Jacques Lacan, *Écrits: The First Complete Edition in English*, trans. Bruce Fink (New York: Norton, 2006), 581 (bracketed insertions in the original).

21. Jacques Lacan, *Speech and Language in Psychoanalysis*, trans. Anthony Wilden (Baltimore: Johns Hopkins University Press, 1968), 187.

22. D. H. Lawrence, *The First and Second Lady Chatterley Novels*, ed. Dieter Mehl and Christa Jansohn (Cambridge: Cambridge University Press, 2002), 439–40. For an extended discussion of this passage, see Masami Nakabayashi, *The Rhetoric of the Unselfconscious in D. H. Lawrence: Verbalising the Non-Verbal in the "Lady Chatterley" Novels* (Lanham, MD: University Press of America, 2011), 137–38.

23. John Marco Allegro, *The Sacred Mushroom and the Cross: A Study of the Nature and Origins of Christianity within the Fertility Cults of the Ancient Near East* (Garden City, NY: Doubleday, 1970).

24. Francis L. Kunkel, *Passion and the Passion: Sex and Religion in Modern Literature* (Philadelphia: Westminster, 1975), 35.

25. Charles Michael Burack, *D. H. Lawrence's Language of Sacred Experience: The Transfiguration of the Reader* (New York: Palgrave Macmillan, 2005), 2.

26. Theodor W. Adorno, *Aesthetic Theory*, ed. Gretel Adorno and Rolf Tiedemann, trans. Robert Hullot-Kentor (Minneapolis: University of Minnesota Press, 1997), 32.

27. Adorno, *Aesthetic Theory*, 33.

28. Theodor W. Adorno, "On Lyric Poetry and Society," in *Notes to Literature* by Adorno, ed. Rolf Tiedemann, trans. Shierry Weber Nicholsen (New York: Columbia University Press, 1991), 1:48.

29. 大考的早晨，那慘淡的心情大概只有軍隊作戰前的黎明可以比擬，像《斯巴達克斯》裏奴隸起義的叛軍在晨霧中遙望羅馬大軍擺陣，所有的戰爭片中最恐怖的一幕，因為完全是等待。Chang, *Xiao tuanyuan*, 18.

30. 不過仍舊一直做夢夢見大考，總是噩夢。Chang, *Xiao tuanyuan*, 18.

31. 墓碑一樣沉重的壓在心上。Chang, *Xiao tuanyuan*, 18.

32. Deborah Tze-lan Sang argues that "Chang calls into question gender and sexual norms" through the failure of the modern girls in her stories. Taking a broader scope, David Der-wei Wang appreciates Chang's humanistic spirit and philosophical insight by pointing out "a bemused look at the contingencies of history and human fate" as the "constant theme of Chang's writings." Deborah Tze-lan Sang, "Eileen Chang and the Genius Art of Failure," in *The Oxford Handbook of Modern Chinese Literatures*, ed. Carlos Rojas and Andrea Bachner (Oxford: Oxford University Press, 2016), 765–78, here 767. David Der-wei Wang, "Madame White, *The Book of Change*, and Eileen Chang: On a Poetics of Involution and Derivation," in *Eileen Chang: Romancing Languages, Cultures and Genres*, ed. Kam Louie (Hong Kong: Hong Kong University Press, 2012), 215–41, here 228. I argue that the sense of failure, negative feelings, or human fate cannot be attributed to a modern gender issue but a human fate that occupies an important domain of literary inquiry in the Chinese tradition.

33. 白銅湯匙; 鐵腥氣 Chang, *Xiao tuanyuan*, 217.

34. 一眼看見就像烙印一樣，再也不會忘記。[. . . . .] 分數燒了，確是像一世功名付之流水。Chang, *Xiao tuanyuan*, 70.

35. 彫刻得非常原始。Chang, *Xiao tuanyuan*, 177.

36. 是遠祖祀奉的偶像？它在看著她。Chang, *Xiao tuanyuan*, 177.

37. 她自己對這些事有一種禁忌，覺得性與生殖與最原始的遠祖之間一脈相傳，是在生命的核心裏的一種神秘與恐怖。Chang, *Xiao tuanyuan*, 319.

38. Chang, *Xiao tuanyuan*, 180.

39. Lanling Xiaoxiao Sheng 蘭陵笑笑生, *The Golden Lotus: A Translation*, trans. F. Clement C. Egerton (London: Routledge & Kegan Paul, 1972), 4.

40. Lanling, *The Golden Lotus*, 2.

41. Xueqin Cao, *The Story of the Stone: A Novel in Five Volumes*, trans. David Hawkes (Bloomington: Indiana University Press, 1979), 12.

42. Cao, *The Story of the Stone*, 53.

43. Zaifu Liu 刘再复, "Eileen Chang's Fiction and C. T. Hsia's *A History of Modern*

Chinese Fiction," in *Liu Zaifu: Selected Critical Essays*, ed. Howard Y. F. Choy and Jianmei Liu (Leiden: Brill, 2021), 297.

44. Chang, *Xiao tuanyuan*, 172.

45. 她覺得過了童年就沒有這樣平安過。Chang, *Xiao tuanyuan*, 172.

46. Chang, *Xiao tuanyuan*, 171–72.

47. Chang, *Xiao tuanyuan*, 189–90.

48. D. H. Lawrence, *Reflections on the Death of a Porcupine and Other Essays*, ed. Michael Herbert (Cambridge: Cambridge University Press, 1988), 300, 299.

49. Frank Kermode, *The Sense of an Ending* (New York: Oxford University Press, 2000 [1967]), 7.

50. Chang, "The Heart Sutra," 45–46. 她的臉是神話裏的小孩的臉 [. . . . .] 有一種奇異的令人不安的美。*Quanji*, 5:245.

51. Chang, "The Heart Sutra," 46. 這裏沒有別的，只有天與上海與小寒。不，天與小寒與上海，因為小寒所坐的地位是介於天與上海之間。*Quanji*, 5:246.

52. From *Xin jing* 心经 (*Heart Sutra*), a Buddhist classic. *Jingang jing, Xin jing, Tan jing* 金刚经·心经·坛经, translated by Qiuping Chen 陈秋平 and Rong Shang 尚荣 (Beijing: Zhonghua shuju, 2007), 89.

53. Chang, "The Heart Sutra," 85. *Quanji*, 5:277.

54. Chang, *Lust, Caution*, 36.

55. Chang, "The Golden Cangue," 190. *Quanji*, 5:53.

56. Chang, *Xiao tuanyuan*, 325.

57. 這是一個熱情故事，我想表達出愛情的萬轉千迴，完全幻滅了之後也還有點什麼東西在。This letter of Chang's is addressed to her close friends and also editors in Taiwan, the Songs, on April 22, 1976. Cited in Yilang Song 宋以朗, "Foreword," in Chang, *Xiao tuanyuan*, 10.

58. Chang, *Written on Water*, 79.

59. Chang, *Quanji*, 8:138.

Conclusion

1. D. H. Lawrence, *The Virgin and the Gipsy and Other Stories*, ed. Michael Herbert, Bethan Jones, and Lindeth Vasey (Cambridge: Cambridge University Press, 2005), 160, 159, 160.

2. Lawrence, *The Virgin and the Gipsy and Other Stories*, 163.

3. Xiaojue Wang, in one of her latest essays, examines Chang's translation of *The Sing-song Girls of Shanghai* to ascertain its unacknowledged value. Chang translated and transformed this classical Chinese literary piece to be intelligible to modern readers. As Wang claims, "Chang sees her role in the textual history of these two books [*The Sing-song Girls of Shanghai* and *Dream of the Red Mansion*]" as the transmitter. See Xiaojue Wang, "Creation and Transmission: Eileen Chang and Sing-song Girls of Shanghai," *Chinese Literature Essays, Articles, Reviews* (CLEAR) 36, no. 4 (2014): 125–48.

4. Eileen Chang (Ailing Zhang 張愛玲), *Written on Water*, ed. Nicole Huang, trans. Andrew F. Jones (New York: Columbia University Press, 2005), 19. 為要證實自己的存在，抓住一點真實的，最基本的東西，不能不求助於古老的記憶，人類在一切時代之中生活過的記憶，這比瞭望將來要更明晰、親切。於是他對於周圍的現實發生了一種奇異的感覺。Eileen Chang (Ailing Zhang 張愛玲), *Zhang Ailing diancang quanji* 張愛玲典藏全集 (*The Complete Works of Zhang Ailing*) (Taipei: Huangguan, 2001), 8:90.

5. Plato, *The Symposium: A New Translation by W. Hamilton*, trans. Walter Hamilton (Harmondsworth: Penguin, 1951), 86.

6. Xianzu Tang 湯顯祖, *The Peony Pavilion* (*Mudan ting* 牡丹亭, 1598), trans. Cyril Birch (Bloomington: Indiana University Press, 2002), ix. This famous Chinese drama recounts the passionate love between Liu Mengmei and Du Liniang.

7. Theodor W. Adorno, *Aesthetic Theory*, ed. Gretel Adorno and Rolf Tiedemann, trans. Robert Hullot-Kentor (Minneapolis: University of Minnesota Press, 1997), 32.

8. Bertrand Russell, "Portraits from Memory: D. H. Lawrence," *Harper's Magazine* 206, no. 1233 (Feb. 1953): 93–95, here 95.

Bibliography

Adams, James. "Victorian Sexualities." In *A Companion to Victorian Literature & Culture*, edited by Herbert F. Tucker, 125–38. Malden, MA: Blackwell, 1999.

Adorno, Theodor W. *Aesthetic Theory*. Edited by Gretel Adorno and Rolf Tiedemann. Translated by Robert Hullot-Kentor. Minneapolis: University of Minnesota Press, 1997.

Adorno, Theodor W. "On Lyric Poetry and Society." In *Notes to Literature*, edited by Rolf Tiedemann, translated by Shierry Weber Nicholsen, 1:37–54. New York: Columbia University Press, 1991.

Ahmed, Sara. *The Cultural Politics of Emotion*. 2nd ed. New York: Routledge, 2015.

Allegro, John Marco. *The Sacred Mushroom and the Cross: A Study of the Nature and Origins of Christianity within the Fertility Cults of the Ancient Near East*. Garden City, NY: Doubleday, 1970.

Appiah, Kwame Anthony. *Cosmopolitanism: Ethics in a World of Strangers*. New York: W. W. Norton, 2006.

Balbert, Peter. *D. H. Lawrence and the Marriage Matrix: Intertextual Adventures in Conflict, Renewal, and Transcendence*. London: Cambridge Scholars, 2016.

Beck, Ulrich. *Cosmopolitan Vision*. Translated by Ciaran Cronin. Cambridge: Polity, 2006.

Belsey, Catherine. *Desire: Love Stories in Western Culture*. Oxford: Blackwell, 1994.

Berlant, Lauren. *Cruel Optimism*. Durham: Duke University Press, 2011.

Black, Michael. *D. H. Lawrence: The Early Fiction: A Commentary*. Basingstoke: Macmillan, 1986.

Black, Michael. *D. H. Lawrence: The Early Philosophical Works*. London: Macmillan, 1991.

Black, Michael. *D. H. Lawrence, Sons and Lovers*. Cambridge: Cambridge University Press, 1992.

Black, Michael. *Lawrence's England: The Major Fiction, 1913–20*. Basingstoke: Palgrave in association with St. Antony's, Oxford, 2001.

Bloom, Harold, ed. *D. H. Lawrence's "Women in Love."* New York: Chelsea House, 1988.

Burack, Charles Michael. *D. H. Lawrence's Language of Sacred Experience: The Transfiguration of the Reader*. New York: Palgrave Macmillan, 2005.

Cai, Dengshan 蔡登山. *Lust, Caution and Eileen Chang* 色戒愛玲. Taipei: INK Publishing, 2007.

Cao, Xueqin. *The Story of the Stone: A Novel in Five Volumes.* Translated by David Hawkes. Bloomington: Indiana University Press, 1979.

Chang, Eileen (Ailing Zhang 張愛玲). "Demons and Fairies." *XX Century* 5, no. 6 (1943): 421–29.

Chang, Eileen (Ailing Zhang 張愛玲). "The Golden Cangue." In *Twentieth-Century Chinese Stories*, edited by Chih-tsing Hsia, 138–91. New York: Columbia University Press, 1971.

Chang, Eileen (Ailing Zhang 張愛玲). "The Heart Sutra." In Roslyn Tom, "The Parent-Child Relationship in Three Stories by Eileen Chang with a Translation of 'The Heart Sutra.'" Master's thesis, Harvard University, 1985.

Chang, Eileen (Ailing Zhang 張愛玲). *Lust, Caution and Other Stories.* Translated by Julia Lovell. London: Penguin, 2007.

Chang, Eileen (Ailing Zhang 張愛玲). "Sealed Off." In *Norton Anthology of World Literature*, edited by Martin Puchner, 1345–54. New York: W.W. Norton, 2012.

Chang, Eileen (Ailing Zhang 張愛玲). "Stale Mates." In *The Longman Anthology of World Literature*, edited by David Damrosch, 745–50. New York: Longman, 2004.

Chang, Eileen (Ailing Zhang 張愛玲). *Written on Water.* Edited by Nicole Huang. Translated by Andrew F. Jones. New York: Columbia University Press, 2005.

Chang, Eileen (Ailing Zhang 張愛玲). *Xiao tuanyuan* 小團圓 (*The Little Reunion*). Taipei: Huangguan, 2009.

Chang, Eileen (Ailing Zhang 張愛玲). *Zhang Ailing diancang quanji* 張愛玲典藏全集 (*The Complete Works of Zhang Ailing*). Vol. 8. Taipei: Huangguan, 2001.

Chang, Sung-sheng Yvonne. "Yuan Qiongqiong and the Rage for Eileen Zhang among Taiwan's 'Feminine' Writers." *Modern Chinese Literature* 4, nos. 1–2 (Spring–Fall 1988): 201–23.

Chen, Zishan 陈子善. *Chenxiang tanxie* 沉香谭屑:张爱玲生平与创作考释 (*Eileen Chang's Life and Works*). Shanghai: Shanghai shudian chubanshe, 2012.

Chen, Zishan 陈子善, ed. *Zhang Ailing de fengqi* 张爱玲的风气:1949 年前张爱玲评说 (*The Characteristics of Eileen Chang*). Ji'nan: Shandong huabao chubanshe, 2004.

Chow, Rey. *Woman and Chinese Modernity: The Politics of Reading between West and East.* Minneapolis: University of Minnesota Press, 1991.

Clarke, Colin. *River of Dissolution: D. H. Lawrence and English Romanticism.* London: Routledge and K. Paul, 1969.

Craig, David. *The Real Foundations: Literature and Social Change.* New York: Oxford University Press, 1974.

Cushman, Keith. "The Virgin and the Gipsy and the Lady and the Gamekeeper." In *D. H. Lawrence's "Lady": A New Look at Lady Chatterley's Lover*, edited by Michael Squires and Dennis Jackson, 154–69. Athens: University of Georgia Press, 1985.

Cushman, Keith, and Dennis Jackson, eds. *D. H. Lawrence's Literary Inheritors.* New York: St. Martin's, 1991.

de Beauvoir, Simone. *The Second Sex.* Translated by H. M. Parshley. New York: Knopf, 1957.

de Rougemont, Denis. "Love." In *Dictionary of the History of Ideas*, vol. 3, edited by Philip Wiener. New York: Scribner, 1973.

de Rougemont, Denis. *Love in the Western World.* New York: Pantheon, 1956.

Denton, Kirk. *Modern Chinese Literary Thought: Writings on Literature, 1893–1945.* Stanford, CA: Stanford University Press, 1996.

Deppman, Hsiu-Chuang. "Seduction of a Filmic Romance." In *Eileen Chang: Romancing Languages, Cultures and Genres*, edited by Kam Louie, 155–76. Hong Kong: Hong Kong University Press, 2012.

Derrida, Jacques. *Of Grammatology*. Translated by Gayatri Chakravorty Spiva. Baltimore: Johns Hopkins University Press, 1974.

Dilley, Whitney Crothers. "The 'Real' Wang Jiazhi: Taboo, Transgression, and Truth in Lust/Caution." In *Eileen Chang to Ang Lee: Lust, Caution*, edited by Xiaoyan Peng and Whitney Crothers Dilley, 121–32. New York: Routledge, 2014.

Doherty, Gerald. "The Nirvana Dimension: D. H. Lawrence's Quarrel with Buddhism." *The D. H. Lawrence Review* 15, nos. 1–2 (1982): 51–76.

Dooling, Amy. *Women's Literary Feminism in Twentieth Century China*. New York: Palgrave Macmillan, 2005.

duCille, Ann. *The Coupling Convention: Sex, Text, and Tradition in Black Women's Fiction*. New York: Oxford University Press, 1993.

Eagleton, Terry. *The English Novel: An Introduction*. Malden, MA: Blackwell, 2005.

Eifring, Halvor. *Love and Emotions in Traditional Chinese Literature*. Leiden: Brill, 2003.

Epstein, Maram. *Competing Discourses: Orthodoxy, Authenticity, and Engendered Meanings in Late Imperial Chinese Fiction*. Cambridge, MA: Harvard University Asia Center, Harvard University Press, 2001.

Featherstone, Mike. "Love and Eroticism: An Introduction." In *Love and Eroticism*, edited by Mike Featherstone, 1–19. London: Sage, 1999.

Fernihough, Anne. *D. H. Lawrence: Aesthetics and Ideology*. Oxford: Clarendon, 1993.

Freud, Sigmund. *On Narcissism: An Introduction*. In *The Standard Edition of the Complete Psychological Works of Sigmund Freud*, edited by James Strachey, 14:67–104. London: Hogarth, 1953–74.

Freud, Sigmund. "On the Universal Tendency to Debasement in the Sphere of Love." In *The Standard Edition of the Complete Psychological Works of Sigmund Freud*, edited by James Strachey, 11:177–90. London: Hogarth, 1953–74.

Freud, Sigmund. "A Special Type of Choice of Object Made by Men." In *The Standard Edition of the Complete Psychological Works of Sigmund Freud*, edited by James Strachey, 11:163–76. London: Hogarth, 1953–74.

Freud, Sigmund. *Three Essays on the Theory of Sexuality*. In *The Standard Edition of the Complete Psychological Works of Sigmund Freud*, edited by James Strachey, 7:123–243. London: Hogarth, 1953–74.

Fromm, Erich. *The Art of Loving*. New York: Harper & Row, 1956.

Green, Eleanor. "Lawrence, Schopenhauer, and the Dual Nature of the Universe." *South Atlantic Bulletin* 62 (Nov. 1977): 84–92.

Green, Eleanor. "Schopenhauer and D. H. Lawrence on Sex and Love." *D. H. Lawrence Review* 8 (Fall 1975): 329–45.

Gregor, Ian, and Brian Nicholas. *The Moral and the Story*. London: Faber and Faber, 1962.

Gu, Ming Dong. "D. H. Lawrence and the Chinese Reader." *The D. H. Lawrence Review* 23, no. 1 (1991): 43–47.

Gu, Ming Dong. "The Filial Piety Complex: The Oedipus Complex in Chinese Cultural Context." In *The Reception and Rendition of Freud in China: China's Freudian Slip*, edited by Tao Jiang and Philip J. Ivanhoe, 60–85. New York: Routledge, 2013.

Gunn, Edward. *Unwelcome Muse: Chinese Literature in Shanghai and Peking (1937–1945)*. New York: Columbia University Press, 1980.

Hanyu da cidian 漢語大詞典. Vol. 5, part 1. Edited by Zhufeng Luo. Shanghai: Hanyu da cidian chubanshe, 2001.

Harrison, Andrew. *D. H. Lawrence: "Sons and Lovers." Literature Insights*. Tirril: Humanities-Ebooks, 2007.

Harvey, Geoffrey. *Sons and Lovers (Critics Debate)*. Atlantic Highlands, NJ: Humanities Press, 1987.

Held, David. "Principles of Cosmopolitan Order." In *The Cosmopolitanism Reader*, edited by Garrett Wallace Brown and David Held, 229–47. Cambridge: Polity, 2010.

Hochman, Baruch. *Another Ego: The Changing View of Self and Society in the Work of D. H. Lawrence*. Columbia: University of South Carolina Press, 1970.

Hoffman, Frederick. *Freudianism and the Literary Mind*. Baton Rouge: Louisiana State University Press, 1957.

Hoffman, Frederick. "Lawrence's Quarrel with Freud." In *The Achievement of D. H. Lawrence*, edited by Frederick Hoffman and Harry T. Moore, 106–27. Norman: University of Oklahoma Press, 1953.

Hsia, C. T. [Chih-tsing]. *A History of Modern Chinese Fiction, 1917–1957*. New Haven: Yale University Press, 1961.

Hsiao-yen, Peng, and Whitney Crothers Dilley, eds. *From Eileen Chang to Ang Lee: Lust/ Caution*. New York: Routledge, 2014.

Hu, Lancheng. *Jinsheng jinshi* 今生今世 (*This Life, These Times*). Beijing: Zhongguo shehui kexue chubanshe, 2003.

Huang, Nicole. *Women, War, Domesticity: Shanghai Literature and Popular Culture of the 1940s*. Leiden: Brill, 2005.

Humma, John B. "The Interpenetrating Metaphor: Nature and Myth in *Lady Chatterley's Lover*." *PMLA* 98, no. 1 (1983): 77–86.

Humma, John B. "Lawrence in Another Light: *Women in Love* and Existentialism." *Studies in the Novel* 24, no. 4 (1992): 392–409.

Ingersoll, Earl G. *D. H. Lawrence, Desire, and Narrative*. Gainesville: University Press of Florida, 2001.

Iwasaki, Clara. *Rethinking the Modern Chinese Canon: Refractions across the Transpacific*. Amherst, NY: Cambria Press, 2020.

Jameson, Fredric. "Third-World Literature in the Era of Multinational Capitalism." *Social Text* 15, no. 3 (1986): 65–88.

Jewinski, Ed. "The Phallus in D. H. Lawrence and Jacques Lacan." *The D. H. Lawrence Review* 21, no. 1 (1989): 7–24.

Jingang jing, Xin jing, Tan jing 金刚经·心经·坛经. Translated by Qiuping Chen 陈秋平 and Rong Shang 尚荣. Beijing: Zhonghua shuju, 2007.

Kant, Immanuel. *Toward Perpetual Peace and Other Writings on Politics, Peace, and History*. Edited by Pauline Kleingeld. Translated by David L. Colclasure. New Haven: Yale University Press, 2006.

Ke, Ling 柯灵. "Yaoji Zhang Ailing" 遥寄张爱玲 (A Letter to Eileen Chang Who Is Far Away). In *Zhang Ailing quanji* 张爱玲全集 (*Complete Works of Eileen Chang*), edited by Hongda Jin and Qing Yu, 947–52. Hefei: Anhui wenyi chubanshe, 1996.

Kermode, Frank. *Lawrence*. London: Fontana/Collins, 1973.

Kermode, Frank. *The Sense of an Ending.* New York: Oxford University Press, 2000 [1967].

Kingsley Widmer. *Defiant Desire: Some Dialectical Legacies of D. H. Lawrence.* Carbondale: Southern Illinois University Press, 1992.

Kunkel, Francis L. *Passion and the Passion: Sex and Religion in Modern Literature.* Philadelphia: Westminster, 1975.

Kuttner, Alfred Booth. "Sons and Lovers: A Freudian Appreciation." *Psychoanalytic Review* 3 (July 1916): 295–317.

Lacan, Jacques. *Écrits: The First Complete Edition in English.* Translated by Bruce Fink. New York: Norton, 2006.

Lacan, Jacques. *Speech and Language in Psychoanalysis.* Translated by Anthony Wilden. Baltimore: Johns Hopkins University Press, 1968.

Lanling Xiaoxiao Sheng 蘭陵笑笑生. *The Golden Lotus: A Translation.* Translated by F. Clement and C. Egerton. London: Routledge & Kegan Paul, 1972.

Larson, Wendy. *From Ah Q to Lei Feng: Freud and Revolutionary Spirit in 20th Century China.* Stanford: Stanford University Press, 2009.

Larson, Wendy. *Women and Writing in Modern China.* Stanford: Stanford University Press, 1998.

Lawrence, D. H. *Apocalypse and the Writings on Revelation.* Edited by Mara Kalnins. London: Cambridge University Press, 1980.

Lawrence, D. H. *The First and Second Lady Chatterley Novels,* Edited by Dieter Mehl and Christa Jansohn. Cambridge: Cambridge University Press, 2002.

Lawrence, D. H. *Lady Chatterley's Lover.* Edited by Michael Squires. Cambridge: Cambridge University Press, 1993.

Lawrence, D. H. *Late Essays and Articles.* Edited by James T. Boulton. Cambridge: Cambridge University Press, 2004.

Lawrence, D. H. *The Letters of D. H. Lawrence, Volume I, September 1901–May 1913.* Edited by James T. Boulton. Cambridge: Cambridge University Press, 1979.

Lawrence, D. H. *The Letters of D. H. Lawrence, Volume II, June 1913–October 1916.* Edited by George J. Zytaruk and James T. Boulton. Cambridge: Cambridge University Press, 2002.

Lawrence, D. H. *The Letters of D. H. Lawrence, Volume VI, March 1927–November 1928.* Edited by James T. Boulton and Margaret Boulton with Gerald M. Lacy. Cambridge: Cambridge University Press, 1991.

Lawrence, D. H. *Psychoanalysis and the Unconscious and Fantasia of the Unconscious.* Edited by Bruce Steele. Cambridge: Cambridge University Press, 2004.

Lawrence, D. H. *Reflections on the Death of a Porcupine and Other Essays.* Edited by Michael Herbert. Cambridge: Cambridge University Press, 1988.

Lawrence, D. H. *Sons and Lovers.* Edited by Helen Baron and Carl Baron. Cambridge: Cambridge University Press, 1992.

Lawrence, D. H. *Study of Thomas Hardy and Other Essays.* Edited by Bruce Steele. Cambridge: Cambridge University Press, 1985.

Lawrence, D. H. *The Virgin and the Gipsy and Other Stories.* Edited by Michael Herbert, Bethan Jones, and Lindeth Vasey. Cambridge: Cambridge University Press, 2005.

Lawrence, D. H. *Women in Love.* Edited by David Farmer, Lindeth Vasey, and John Worthen. Cambridge: Cambridge University Press, 1987.

Leavis, F. R. *D. H. Lawrence: Novelist*. New York: Simon & Schuster, 1969.

Lee, Ang. "Afterword." In *Lust, Caution: The Story* by Eileen Chang. New York: Anchor, 2007.

Lee, Haiyan. "Eileen Chang's Poetics of the Social: Review of *Love in a Fallen City*." *Modern Chinese Literature and Culture* (MCLC) Resource Center, Ohio State University, 2007. http://u.osu.edu/mclc/book-reviews/review-of-love-in-a-fallen-city/

Lee, Haiyan. "Enemy under My Skin: Eileen Chang's *Lust, Caution* and the Politics of Transcendence." *PMLA* 125, no. 3 (2010): 640–56.

Lee, Haiyan. *Revolution of the Heart: A Genealogy of Love in China, 1900–1950*. Stanford: Stanford University Press, 2007.

Lee, Leo Ou-fan. *Cangliang yu shigu: Zhang Ailing de qishi* 蒼涼與世故：張愛玲的啟示 (*Desolation and Sophistication*). Hong Kong: Oxford University Press, 2006.

Lee, Leo Ou-fan. *Shanghai Modern: The Flowering of a New Urban Culture in China, 1930–1945*. Cambridge, MA: Harvard University Press, 1999.

Lee, Tong King. "Forbidden Imaginations: Three Chinese Narratives on Mother-Son Incest." *Chinese Literature Essays, Articles, Reviews* (*CLEAR*) 36, no. 4 (2014): 1–24.

Lerner, Laurence. "Lawrence and the Feminists." In *D. H. Lawrence: Centenary Essays*, edited by Mara Kalnins, 69–88. Bristol: Bristol Classical, 1986.

Levi-Strauss, Claude. *The Elementary Structures of Kinship*. Edited by Rodney Needham. Translated by James Harle Bell, John Richard von Sturmer, and Rodney Needham. Boston: Beacon, 1969.

Lewis, C. S. *The Allegory of Love: A Study in Medieval Tradition*. Oxford: Clarendon, 1936.

Lewis, C. S. *The Four Loves*. London: Geoffrey Bles, 1960.

Lin, Xingqian 林幸謙, ed. *Zhang Ailing: Wenxue, dianying, wutai* 張愛玲：文學·電影·舞台 (*Eileen Chang: Literature, Film, and the Stage*). Hong Kong: Oxford University Press, 2007.

Link, Perry. "Mao's China: The Language Game." *New York Review of Books*, 15 May 2015.

Liu, Xianzhi. "Lawrence in China: The Reception of D. H. Lawrence in China." *The D. H. Lawrence Review* 23, no. 1 (1991): 37–55.

Liu, Zaifu 刘再复. "Eileen Chang's Fiction and C. T. Hsia's *A History of Modern Chinese Fiction*." In *Liu Zaifu: Selected Critical Essays*, 294–327. Leiden: Brill, 2021.

Lovell, Julia. "Editor's Afterword." In *Lust, Caution and Other Stories* by Eileen Chang. Edited by Julia Lovell. London: Penguin, 2007.

Lu, Tonglin. *Gender and Sexuality in Twentieth-Century Chinese Literature and Society*. Albany: State University of New York Press, 1993.

Luhmann, Niklas. *Love as Passion: The Codification of Intimacy*. Translated by Jeremy Gaines. Cambridge, MA: Harvard University Press, 1987.

McDougall, Bonnie S. *Mao Zedong's "Talks at the Yan'an Conference on Literature and Art": A Translation of the 1943 Text with Commentary*. Ann Arbor: University of Michigan Center for Chinese Studies, 1980.

Millet, David. *National Responsibility and Global Justice*. Oxford: Oxford University Press, 2007.

Millett, Kate. *Sexual Politics*. Garden City, NY: Doubleday, 1970.

Milne, Drew. "Lawrence and the Politics of Sexual Politics." In *The Cambridge Companion to D. H. Lawrence*, edited by Anne Fernihough, 197–216. Cambridge: Cambridge University Press, 2001.

Milton, Colin. *Lawrence and Nietzsche: A Study in Influence*. Aberdeen: Aberdeen University Press, 1987.

Moretti, Franco. "Conjectures on World Literature." *New Left Review* 1 (Jan.–Feb. 2000): 54–68.

Nakabayashi, Masami. *The Rhetoric of the Unselfconscious in D. H. Lawrence: Verbalising the Non-Verbal in the "Lady Chatterley" Novels*. Lanham, MD: University Press of America, 2011.

Nietzsche, Friedrich. *The Birth of Tragedy and the Genealogy of Morals*. Translated by Francis Golffing. New York: Anchor, 1990.

Nussbaum, Martha C. *For Love of Country*. Edited by Joshua Cohen. Boston: Beacon, 1996.

Nussbaum, Martha C. "Kant and Cosmopolitanism." In *Perpetual Peace: Essays on Kant's Cosmopolitan Ideal*, edited by James Bohmann and Matthias Lutz-Bachmann, 25–57. Cambridge, MA: MIT Press, 1997.

Nussbaum, Martha C. "Toward a Globally Sensitive Patriotism." *Daedalus* 137, no. 3 (Summer 2008): 78–93.

Panken, Shirley. "Some Psychodynamics in *Sons and Lovers*: A New Look at the Oedipal Theme." *Psychoanalytic Review* 61, no. 4 (1974): 571–89.

Paxton, Nancy. "Reimagining Melodrama: *The Virgin and the Gipsy* and the Consequences of Mourning." *The D. H. Lawrence Review* 38, no. 2 (2013): 58–76.

Pitre, David. "The Mystical Lawrence: Rupert Birkin's Taoist Quest." *Studies in Mystical Literature* 3, no. 1 (1983): 43–64.

Plaks, Andrew. "The Problem of Incest in *Jin Ping Mei* and *Honglou meng*." In *Paradoxes of Traditional Chinese Literature*, edited by Eva Hung, 123–46. Hong Kong: Chinese University Press, 1994.

Plato, *The Symposium: A New Translation by W. Hamilton*. Translated by Walter Hamilton. Harmondsworth: Penguin, 1951.

Porter, David. *Ideographia: The Chinese Cipher in Early Modern Europe*. Stanford: Stanford University Press, 2001.

Reed, John Robert. *Victorian Conventions*. Athens: Ohio University Press, 1975.

Russell, Bertrand. "Portraits from Memory: D. H. Lawrence." *Harper's Magazine* 206, no. 1233 (Feb. 1953): 93–95.

Salgādo, Gāmini. *D. H. Lawrence: Sons and Lovers*. London: Macmillan, 1969.

Sang, Deborah Tze-lan. "Eileen Chang and the Genius Art of Failure." In *The Oxford Handbook of Modern Chinese Literatures*, edited by Carlos Rojas and Andrea Bachner, 765–78. Oxford: Oxford University Press, 2016.

Sang, Deborah Tze-lan. "Romancing Rhetoricity and Historicity: The Representational Politics and Poetics of *Little Reunion*." In *Eileen Chang: Romancing Languages, Cultures and Genres*, edited by Kam Louie, 193–213. Hong Kong: Hong Kong University Press, 2012.

Saussy, Haun. *Great Walls of Discourse and Other Adventures in Cultural China*. Cambridge, MA: Harvard University Press, 2001.

Shen, Shuang, ed. *Lingdu kan Zhang* 零度看張 (*Eileen Chang Degree Zero*). Hong Kong: Chinese University Press, 2012.

Shih, Shu-mei. "World Studies and Relational Comparison." *PMLA* 130, no. 2 (2015): 430–38.

Shui, Jing 水晶. *Zhang Ailing de xiaoshuo yishu* 張愛玲的小說藝術 (*The Art of Eileen Chang's Fiction*). Taipei: Dadi, 1973.

Shumway, David R. *Modern Love: Romance, Intimacy, and the Marriage Crisis*. New York: New York University Press, 2003.

Siegel, Carol. "Floods of Female Desire in Lawrence and Eudora Welty." In *D. H. Lawrence's Literary Inheritors*, edited by Keith Cushman and Dennis Jackson, 109–30. New York: St. Martin's, 1991.

Simpson, Hilary. *D. H. Lawrence and Feminism*. DeKalb: Northern Illinois University Press, 1982.

Singer, Irving. *The Nature of Love*. Chicago: University of Chicago Press, 1984.

Song, Yilang 宋以朗. "Foreword." In *Xiao tuanyuan* 小團圓 (*The Little Reunion*) by Eileen Chang (Ailing Zhang 張愛玲). Taipei: Huangguan, 2009.

Spilka, Mark. "Counterfeit Loves." In *Twentieth Century Interpretations of Sons and Lovers: A Collection of Critical Essays*, edited by Judith Farr, 51–63. Englewood Cliffs, NJ: Prentice-Hall, 1970.

Spilka, Mark. *The Love Ethic of D. H. Lawrence*. Bloomington: Indiana University Press, 1966.

Stewart, Kathleen. *Ordinary Affects*. Durham: Duke University Press, 2007.

Tang, Wenbiao 唐文標. *Zhang Ailing ziliao daquanji* 張愛玲資料大全集 (*The Complete Collection of Materials of Eileen Chang*). Taipei: Shibao wenhua chuban shiye youxian gongsi, 1984.

Tang, Xianzu 湯顯祖. *The Peony Pavilion* (*Mudan ting* 牡丹亭, 1598). Translated by Cyril Birch. Bloomington: Indiana University Press, 2002.

Tindall, William York. "Transcendentalism in Contemporary Literature." In *The Asian Legacy and American Life*, edited by Arthur Christy, 175–92. New York: John Day, 1945.

Turner, John. "Purity and Danger in D. H. Lawrence's *The Virgin and the Gipsy*." In *D. H. Lawrence: Centenary Essays*, edited by Mara Kalnins, 139–72. Bristol: Bristol Classical, 1986.

Urang, Sarah. *Kindled in the Flame: The Apocalyptic Scene in D. H. Lawrence*. Ann Arbor, MI: UMI Research, 1983.

Wang, David Der-wei. "Madame White, *The Book of Change*, and Eileen Chang: On a Poetics of Involution and Derivation." In *Eileen Chang: Romancing Languages, Cultures and Genres*, edited by Kam Louie, 215–41. Hong Kong: Hong Kong University Press, 2012.

Wang, Xiaojue. "Creation and Transmission: Eileen Chang and *Sing-song Girls of Shanghai*." *Chinese Literature Essays, Articles, Reviews* (*CLEAR*) 36, no. 4 (2014): 125–48.

Watson, Garry. "'The Fact, and the Crucial Significance, of Desire': Lawrence's 'Virgin and the Gipsy.'" *English* 34 (Summer 1985): 131–56.

Weiss, Daniel A. "The Mother in the Mind." In *Twentieth Century Interpretations of Sons and Lovers: A Collection of Critical Essays*, edited by Judith Farr, 28–41. Englewood Cliffs, NJ: Prentice-Hall, 1970.

Whelan, P. T. *D. H. Lawrence: Myth and Metaphysic in The Rainbow and Women in Love*. Ann Arbor, MI: UMI Research, 1988.

Williams, Linda Ruth. *D. H. Lawrence*. Plymouth, UK: Northcote House in Association with the British Council, 1997.

Xiao, Jiwei. "Belated Reunion? Eileen Chang, Late Style and World Literature." *New Left Review* 111 (May-June 2018): 89–110.

Yao, Sijia. "The Politics of Literary Fame: Tracing Eileen Chang's Reception in China and the United States." *Forum for World Literature Studies* 8, no. 2 (2016): 291–307.

Yao, Sijia. "Third Term Comparison." *Telos* 199 (Summer 2022): 11–19.

Zamperini, Paola. "A Family Romance: Specters of Incest in Eileen Chang's 'Xinjing.'" *Prism: Theory and Modern Chinese Literature* 17, no. 1 (March 2020): 1–34.

Zhang, Chunjie. "Introduction: Latour's Compositionism and Global Modernism." In *Composing Modernist Connections in China and Europe*, edited by Chunjie Zhang, 1–11. New York: Routledge, 2019.

Zhang, Jingyuan. *Psychoanalysis in China: Literary Transformations 1919–1949*. Ithaca, NY: Cornell East Asia Series, Cornell University, 1992.

Zhang, Xiaohong 張小虹. *Wenben Zhang Ailing* 文本張愛玲 (*Textualizing Eileen Chang*). Taipei: Shibao wenhua chuban qiye gufen youxian gongsi, 2020.

Index

women: adultery and women's power, 88–89; Confucian moral principles for women, 63; criticism of women writers in China, 136n34; darkness of, 67; desolation as feminine, 92; female desire in "Lust, Caution" (Chang), 56–58, 60–61, 65–67, 68; female desire in *The Little Reunion* (Chang), 58; female desire in *The Virgin and the Gipsy* (Lawrence), 53–56, 60–63, 65–66, 67, 68; as spies, 63

Women in Love (Lawrence): Chinese translations, 128n70; scholarship on, 95–96; suicide in, 61, 96; utopia and

transcendence in, 29, 95–100, 110–12, 118

"Writing of One's Own" (Chang), 1, 80–81, 91, 119

Written on Water (Chang), 13

Xiao tuanyuan (Chang). See *The Little Reunion* (Chang)

"Xin jing" (Chang). *See* "The Heart Sutra" (Chang)

Xi Shi, 63

Yu, Dafu, 35

Zamperini, Paola, 48, 131n49

Printed and bound by CPI Group (UK) Ltd, Croydon, CR0 4YY

09/06/2025

14686131-0001